# Digital Transformation of SAP Supply Chain Processes

## Build Mobile Apps Using SAP BTP and SAP Mobile Services

Pranay Gupta

**Apress®**

*Digital Transformation of SAP Supply Chain Processes: Build Mobile Apps Using SAP BTP and SAP Mobile Services*

Pranay Gupta
Atlanta, GA, United States

ISBN-13 (pbk): 979-8-8688-0269-0 ISBN-13 (electronic): 979-8-8688-0270-6
https://doi.org/10.1007/979-8-8688-0270-6

Managing Director, Apress Media LLC: Welmoed Spahr
Acquisitions Editor: James Robinson Prior
Development Editor: James Markham
Editorial Assistant: Gryffin Winkler
Copy Editor: Kezia Endsley

Cover designed by eStudioCalamar

Cover image designed by Freepik (www.freepik.com)

Distributed to the book trade worldwide by Springer Science+Business Media New York, 1 New York Plaza, Suite 4600, New York, NY 10004-1562, USA. Phone 1-800-SPRINGER, fax (201) 348-4505, e-mail orders-ny@springer-sbm.com, or visit www.springeronline.com. Apress Media, LLC is a California LLC and the sole member (owner) is Springer Science + Business Media Finance Inc (SSBM Finance Inc). SSBM Finance Inc is a **Delaware** corporation.

For information on translations, please e-mail booktranslations@springernature.com; for reprint, paperback, or audio rights, please e-mail bookpermissions@springernature.com.

Apress titles may be purchased in bulk for academic, corporate, or promotional use. eBook versions and licenses are also available for most titles. For more information, reference our Print and eBook Bulk Sales web page at http://www.apress.com/bulk-sales.

Any source code or other supplementary material referenced by the author in this book is available to readers on GitHub. For more detailed information, please visit https://www.apress.com/gp/services/source-code.

Paper in this product is recyclable

*In the pursuit of knowledge and the
creation of this book, I am profoundly grateful
for the unwavering support and love of two
extraordinary individuals—my beloved wife Sugandh
and our cherished son Ivyaan.*

*Sugandh, you have been the anchor in the
storm of deadlines and challenges, a source of
unwavering encouragement, and the silent force
that kept me going. Your understanding, patience,
and belief in my endeavors have been the cornerstone
of this project. Your sacrifices and tireless support are the
foundation upon which this book stands.*

*To my dear Ivyaan, your infectious laughter,
boundless energy, and innocent curiosity have been a
constant reminder of the importance of the work I do.
Your presence has turned even the most demanding
moments into opportunities for growth and inspiration.
This book is a tribute to the joy you bring into our lives and
a promise to continue striving for a better future for you.*

*Together, you both have been my motivation,
my solace, and my greatest cheerleaders. This book is
not just a professional accomplishment; it is a shared
victory made possible by the love and support that
envelops our family.*

*With heartfelt gratitude and immense love,*

*Pranay*

# Table of Contents

viii

# About the Author

**Pranay Gupta** is a senior advisory consultant at IBM with over 18 years of dedicated experience in the ever-evolving realm of technology and enterprise solutions. He is a certified project management professional (PMP). His proficiency in SAP is further underscored by a series of certifications, including SAP S/4HANA Sourcing and Procurement, S/4HANA EWM (Extended Warehouse Management), ARIBA Buying and Invoicing, and SAP SRM (Supplier Relationship Management). His passion for innovation has led him to explore the synergies between mobility and SAP, enhancing the efficiency and accessibility of enterprise processes. He has been instrumental in providing strategic guidance and solutions to a diverse set of industries, including oil and gas, manufacturing, telecom, travel, and transportation. This wide-ranging exposure has allowed him to understand and address the unique needs and intricacies of each sector, contributing to their growth and digital transformation of ERP processes. He has a keen interest in exploring cloud technologies and he is an Amazon Certified AWS Cloud Professional and a Microsoft Certified Azure Cloud Professional.

# About the Technical Reviewer

 With 15 years of IT experience in ERP solutions, **Sugandh Gupta** is a seasoned Salesforce consultant. Her expertise encompasses a wide range of areas within Salesforce, including implementation, customization, and optimization, and she has demonstrated her skills in utilizing various APIs to enhance and streamline Salesforce implementations, ensuring smooth connectivity with external systems and data sources. Sugandh's technical proficiency extends beyond standard Salesforce configurations, showcasing a deep understanding of API-based solutions.

# Introduction

This book offers a paradigm shift in the execution of SAP transactions, as it explores the use of iOS apps rather than traditional desktop interfaces or SAP's native Fiori apps. Specifically designed for scenarios where clients seek alternatives to SAP's Fiori apps for SAP supply chain or other modules, this book provides a roadmap for modernizing and streamlining supply chain operations through the innovative utilization of Angular iOS apps.

Key highlights include understanding the intricacies of integrating SAP's backend (SAP ECC) with Angular iOS apps using SAP Mobile Services on SAP BTP. Readers will gain insights into high-level SAP supply chain processes, the process of linking Zebra printers to iOS for SAP PDF label printing, and fundamental procedures for setting up authorization endpoints, token endpoints, virus scanning, and base URLs within SAP Mobile Services.

The book explores essential knowledge on managing attachments in mobile applications and storing them in an external content repository by leveraging SAP Document Management System (DMS) configurations. The book also guides readers in acquiring proficiency in testing OData services using the POSTMAN API client with the OAuth protocol. It also helps readers understand JSON messages, the CORS protocol, and X-CSRF tokens in data exchange.

This book is not just a manual; it is a compass for businesses aiming to remain competitive in today's technology-driven landscape. Readers will gain the expertise needed to navigate the evolving landscape of SAP integrations, enhance supply chain processes, and embrace the future of digital transformation.

# CHAPTER 1

# Growing Need of Mobility Apps for ERP Solutions

In the modern business landscape, where agility, accessibility, and real-time decision-making are paramount, integrating mobile applications into SAP (Systems, Applications, and Products) ERP (Enterprise Resource Planning) solutions has emerged as an imperative. This transformational shift signifies a pivotal moment in how organizations leverage technology to optimize operations, engage users, and drive a competitive advantage.

## The Evolution of SAP Mobility

The journey toward SAP Mobility has been a progressive one, reflecting the evolving needs of businesses. Traditionally, ERP systems were confined to desktop environments, limiting accessibility and flexibility. However, the advent of smartphones and tablets ushered in a new era, empowering users to interact with ERP systems from virtually anywhere.

This evolution has led to the recognition of the critical role that mobile applications play in augmenting SAP ERP solutions. These applications serve as a bridge between traditional ERP systems and the dynamic,

© Pranay Gupta 2024
P. Gupta, *Digital Transformation of SAP Supply Chain Processes,*
https://doi.org/10.1007/979-8-8688-0270-6_1

on-the-go nature of today's workforce. They empower users to perform tasks, access information, and make informed decisions in real-time, regardless of their physical location.

# Benefits of Mobile Applications for SAP ERP

Mobile applications in SAP ERP solutions are driven by a multitude of benefits:

1. **Enhanced accessibility:** Mobile applications offer a transformative advantage in terms of enhanced accessibility. They break down the traditional barriers of location and time, allowing users to access critical ERP data and functionalities from virtually anywhere, at any time. This accessibility is particularly valuable to field service personnel, sales teams, executives, and any employees who require instant access to crucial business information. Mobile apps empower users to perform tasks, make decisions, and collaborate with colleagues while on the go. Whether it's checking inventory levels, processing purchase orders, or reviewing sales figures, the ability to access ERP data remotely fosters agility and responsiveness within the organization. It ensures that employees are not tied to their desks and can remain productive even when they are outside the office. As a result, businesses can streamline their operations, reduce delays, and make informed decisions without the constraints of physical location. Furthermore, enhanced accessibility extends beyond the corporate office, enabling companies to connect with global

partners, suppliers, and customers seamlessly. This capability not only enhances internal workflows but also strengthens external relationships, driving efficiency and customer satisfaction.

2. **Improved productivity:** Mobile applications are powerful tools for boosting productivity within an organization. These apps streamline processes, reduce the need for manual data entry, and provide intuitive interfaces that simplify complex tasks. As a result, users can perform their roles more efficiently, leading to faster decision-making and a reduction in operational bottlenecks. With mobile apps, employees can access and update critical data in real-time, eliminating the delays associated with manual data synchronization. This real-time access ensures that everyone is working with the most current information, reducing the risk of errors and improving data accuracy. The intuitive interfaces of mobile apps minimize the learning curve for new users and enhance user adoption. Employees can quickly become proficient in using the apps, allowing them to focus on their core responsibilities rather than wrestling with complicated software. In addition, mobile apps often come with features that automate routine tasks, such as data capture through the device's camera or barcode scanning. These features reduce the time and effort required for data entry and minimize the chances of data entry errors. As a result, employees can accomplish more in less time, leading to increased overall productivity.

3.  **Real-time insights:** Mobile applications provide
    stakeholders with a valuable benefit—real-time
    insights into business operations. These apps enable
    users to receive instant updates on key metrics,
    such as inventory levels, sales figures, production
    status, and financial data. This timely access to
    critical information empowers decision-makers
    to make data-driven decisions promptly and
    effectively. Real-time insights are particularly vital
    in a fast-paced business environment where market
    conditions, customer preferences, and competitive
    landscapes can change rapidly. With mobile apps,
    executives, managers, and employees can stay
    informed about changes as they occur, allowing
    them to adapt strategies and tactics accordingly. For
    example, a sales manager can monitor daily sales
    performance through a mobile app, identifying
    trends and responding to fluctuations in demand.
    Similarly, a production manager can track machine
    uptime and production rates in real-time, making
    immediate adjustments to optimize output. Real-
    time insights facilitate proactive problem-solving
    and enable organizations to seize opportunities
    as they arise. Whether it's responding to a sudden
    surge in customer orders or addressing supply chain
    disruptions, mobile apps equip businesses with
    the agility needed to stay competitive in dynamic
    markets.

4.  **User engagement:** Mobile applications are
    designed with user engagement in mind, making
    ERP systems more approachable and user-friendly.
    This enhanced user engagement is a significant
    benefit, as engaged users are more likely to embrace
    technology and maximize its potential. The user-
    centric design of mobile ERP apps focuses on
    delivering an intuitive and visually appealing user
    interface. This design approach simplifies complex
    ERP processes, making them more accessible to
    a broader range of employees. Users can quickly
    navigate the app, access relevant information, and
    perform tasks without requiring extensive training
    or technical expertise. Engaged users tend to be
    more proactive and self-reliant, reducing the burden
    on IT support teams. They are more likely to explore
    the app's features, discover new ways to optimize
    their workflows, and suggest improvements or
    enhancements. Furthermore, mobile ERP apps
    often offer features that enhance collaboration
    and communication. Employees can easily share
    information, exchange messages, and collaborate
    on projects directly through the app. This fosters a
    sense of community and teamwork, driving higher
    levels of engagement and job satisfaction among
    employees. Ultimately, user engagement leads
    to increased adoption of mobile ERP apps and a
    more productive workforce, contributing to the
    organization's overall success.

5. **Competitive advantage:** Mobile applications confer a distinct competitive advantage to organizations. By leveraging these apps, businesses can respond more rapidly to market changes, evolving customer demands, and emerging opportunities. This agility becomes a game-changer in today's fast-paced business environment, where the ability to adapt swiftly is a key determinant of success. Mobile apps enable organizations to stay ahead of the competition by facilitating quicker decision-making. With real-time access to critical data and insights, leaders can identify market trends, customer preferences, and competitive threats promptly. This early awareness allows businesses to adjust their strategies, refine their products or services, and seize new opportunities before competitors can react. Additionally, mobile apps enhance customer engagement and satisfaction. Sales and customer service teams can provide faster responses to customer inquiries, address issues promptly, and offer personalized experiences. This results in higher customer retention rates and increased loyalty, which can be a significant competitive advantage. The competitive edge gained through mobile apps extends to operational efficiency as well. Improved productivity, streamlined processes, and reduced errors contribute to cost savings and a more agile business model.

# Need for Custom Apps and Associated Challenges

Customizing apps when a client is not satisfied with native Fiori apps provided by SAP can be a complex and strategic decision. Here are some details to consider:

1. **Understanding client needs:** The foundation of any successful custom app development effort in the realm of SAP Mobility is a deep understanding of the client's specific requirements and pain points. This initial step is akin to laying the groundwork for the entire project. It involves engaging in a comprehensive dialogue with the client to unearth their unique needs and challenges within their SAP environment. Start by listening attentively to your client's objectives and concerns. What are the precise features or functionalities that are currently missing in the native Fiori apps that they require? It's essential to drill down into the specifics to identify the pain points and bottlenecks that hinder their productivity. Perhaps they need enhanced reporting capabilities, real-time integration with external systems, or custom workflows tailored to their unique business processes. This phase of understanding the client's needs goes beyond surface-level inquiries. It necessitates collaboration with various stakeholders within the client's organization to capture a holistic view of their requirements. By doing this, you gain insights into not only what they need but also why they need

it. Understanding the "why" is pivotal to crafting solutions that are not just functional but also strategically aligned with the client's overarching business objectives.

2.  **Assessing the native Fiori apps:** Before embarking on the path of custom app development, a thorough assessment of the native Fiori apps provided by SAP that your client finds unsatisfactory is crucial. This assessment serves as the diagnostic phase of the project, where you pinpoint the specific areas of dissatisfaction and the reasons behind them. Begin by conducting a detailed evaluation of the native Fiori apps in question. Identify the aspects that are causing the client's dissatisfaction. Is it due to a lack of customization options within these apps, or are there inherent limitations in the native apps themselves? Are there gaps in functionality, user experience, or integration that hinder the client's ability to perform their tasks efficiently? This phase involves scrutinizing the native apps from various angles, including usability, functionality, performance, and scalability. By comprehensively assessing the native Fiori apps, you gain a clearer picture of the challenges that need to be addressed. It also helps in determining whether customization, enhancement, or the development of entirely new custom apps is the most appropriate path forward.

3.  **Choosing customization vs. development:** The decision to pursue customization of existing Fiori apps or embark on the development of entirely new custom apps is a pivotal one in the project's

lifecycle. It hinges on the extent of the required changes and the alignment with the client's goals. Customization often proves to be a more cost-effective and time-efficient approach when the required modifications are relatively minor. It involves tailoring existing Fiori apps to better align with the client's needs. Customization can encompass changes to user interfaces, data presentation, workflows, and even the addition of new features within the framework of the native apps. Conversely, in cases where the client's needs demand substantial alterations or entirely new functionalities that are not feasible within the confines of the native apps, custom app development becomes a necessity. This path offers the flexibility to build apps from the ground up, ensuring that they are precisely aligned with the client's requirements. The decision between customization and development should be based on a cost-benefit analysis, considering factors such as project timelines, budget constraints, and the long-term scalability of the solution. It's a strategic choice that sets the project's direction and shapes the ultimate deliverables.

4. **Exploring SAP Fiori extensibility options:**
   SAP Fiori offers a range of extensibility options, including the SAP Fiori Elements framework, which simplifies the customization of existing apps. These options provide a middle ground between full custom development and native app usage, and they should be explored thoroughly during the

project's planning phase. The SAP Fiori Elements framework, for instance, enables developers to enhance existing apps by adding custom fields, modifying layouts, and extending the application's functionality. This approach leverages the native app's foundation while tailoring it to the client's specific needs. It's a particularly attractive option when the required changes can be achieved without significant development efforts. Exploring SAP Fiori's extensibility options should be an integral part of the project's strategy, as these options can potentially provide solutions that address the client's requirements without the need for extensive custom development. This approach often offers the benefits of faster implementation and ongoing compatibility with SAP updates.

5. **Considering user experience design:** Whether you opt for customization or custom app development, user experience design should be a central focus. Custom apps need to provide an intuitive and efficient user interface that aligns seamlessly with the client's brand and workflow. Effective user experience design begins by understanding how users interact with the app and the workflows they engage in. This insight informs the creation of user interfaces that prioritize ease of use, minimize cognitive load, and enhance user productivity. User-centric design principles guide the development of custom apps, ensuring that they are not just functional but also a pleasure to use. Elements such as navigation menus, data

presentation, input forms, and interactive elements should be designed with the end user in mind. Considering accessibility and responsive design is also crucial to accommodate diverse user needs and devices. A well-designed user interface fosters user adoption, reduces training overhead, and enhances overall satisfaction with the app. It also contributes to the app's long-term success, as users are more likely to engage with and rely on an app that is user-friendly.

6. **Integrating with SAP Systems:** In the context of SAP Mobility, custom apps, if developed, must seamlessly integrate with the client's existing SAP landscape. This integration encompasses multiple dimensions, including compatibility with SAP modules, data sources, and adherence to SAP's security protocols. Integration with SAP modules ensures that the custom app can access and manipulate relevant data and functionalities within the SAP ecosystem. This may involve connecting with SAP's various modules, such as SAP S/4HANA, SAP ECC, or SAP Business Suite, depending on the client's configuration. Data integration is another critical aspect. Custom apps need to pull and push data to and from SAP systems in real-time or near-real-time to ensure data accuracy and consistency. Integration mechanisms may include APIs, web services, or middleware solutions to facilitate data flow. Security is paramount in SAP environments, and custom apps must adhere to SAP's security protocols and standards. This includes user

authentication, authorization, encryption, and compliance with data privacy regulations. Ensuring the security of sensitive data within the app is essential to prevent data breaches or compliance violations.

7. **Handling data management and security:**
   Data management and security are paramount considerations when developing custom apps for SAP Mobility. Addressing these concerns ensures the confidentiality, integrity, and availability of sensitive data while maintaining compliance with data privacy regulations. Custom apps must be designed to handle data securely, whether it's financial records, customer information, or proprietary business data. Robust data encryption mechanisms should be in place to protect data during transmission and storage. Role-based access control should be implemented to restrict data access to authorized users only, aligning with SAP's security protocols. Compliance with data privacy regulations, such as GDPR (General Data Protection Regulation) or HIPAA (Health Insurance Portability and Accountability Act), is critical. The custom app should be configured to manage personal data in compliance with the relevant regulations, including data consent management and the ability to fulfill data subject access requests. Addressing data management and security concerns not only safeguards sensitive information but also fosters trust among users and ensures legal compliance.

8. **Ensuring scalability and performance:** The need for custom apps in SAP Mobility extends to ensuring scalability and performance. Organizations often grow and evolve, and custom apps should be designed to accommodate these changes. Scalability refers to the app's ability to handle growing user loads and data volumes without a significant drop in performance. Scalability planning begins by considering the expected user base and data growth over time. Custom apps should be architected in a way that allows them to scale horizontally or vertically as needed. This could involve deploying additional server resources, optimizing database structures, or implementing caching mechanisms to enhance performance. Performance optimization is equally important. Custom apps should remain responsive, even under heavy use. This involves optimizing database queries, minimizing network latency, and fine-tuning code to ensure swift execution. Load testing and performance profiling are essential steps to identify and rectify potential bottlenecks before they impact users. Scalability and performance considerations are future-proofing measures that help ensure the long-term viability of custom apps as an organization's needs evolve.

9. **Testing and quality assurance:** Implementing a rigorous testing and quality assurance (QA) process is a non-negotiable aspect of custom app development for SAP Mobility. Thorough testing aims to identify and rectify any issues, bugs, or usability problems before deploying the app to

users. The testing phase encompasses various dimensions, including functional testing to ensure that all features work as intended, usability testing to evaluate the user experience, compatibility testing across different devices and browsers, and security testing to identify vulnerabilities. Load testing and performance testing are crucial for assessing how the app performs under various conditions, including heavy user loads. This type of testing helps uncover scalability and performance issues that may need to be addressed. A well-executed QA process ensures that the custom app meets the defined requirements and aligns with user expectations. It minimizes the risk of post-launch disruptions and enhances the overall quality of the solution.

10. **Providing documentation and training:** Providing comprehensive documentation and conducting training sessions are essential for ensuring a smooth transition to custom apps in SAP Mobility. Documentation should include user guides, admin manuals, and technical documentation for developers. User guides help end users understand how to navigate and use the app effectively. Admin manuals assist administrators in managing and maintaining the app, including user access and data management. Training sessions are critical for both end users and administrators. End users should receive training on how to use the app, its features, and any new workflows it introduces. Administrators need training on managing user

accounts, handling data, and troubleshooting common issues. Effective documentation and training contribute to user adoption and minimize disruptions during the transition to custom apps.

11. **Providing support and maintenance:** Establishing a support and maintenance plan is essential for addressing any issues, updates, or enhancements that may arise after deploying custom apps. A robust support mechanism ensures that the app remains operational and responsive to changing needs. Support should include a helpdesk or support team that can address user queries and technical issues promptly. A ticketing system can help track and prioritize support requests, ensuring efficient problem resolution. Maintenance involves applying updates, patches, and enhancements to the app. Regular maintenance ensures that the app remains compatible with evolving SAP systems and operating environments. It also provides an opportunity to address any identified issues or improve the app's performance. The goal of support and maintenance is to provide a reliable and responsive experience for app users and administrators, contributing to long-term satisfaction and effectiveness.

12. **Establishing the budget and timeline:** Clear definition of the project budget and timeline is crucial for managing expectations and ensuring the project's success. Customization or development of apps can be time-consuming and may require a substantial investment, so it's important to have a well-defined

plan. Budget considerations should encompass development costs, testing expenses, licensing fees, and ongoing support and maintenance expenses. It's essential to factor in possible contingencies and unexpected costs to avoid budget overruns. Project timelines should outline key milestones, including requirements gathering, development phases, testing, and deployment. A well-managed timeline ensures that the project progresses smoothly and aligns with the client's expectations. Managing the budget and timeline effectively helps prevent project delays and cost overruns, ensuring the successful delivery of custom apps.

13. **Implementing change management:**
Implementing a change management strategy is crucial to facilitate user adoption of the new or customized apps. Change management addresses resistance to change and communicates the benefits of the solution to stakeholders. Start by identifying key stakeholders and involving them in the process from the early stages. Communicate the rationale behind the custom apps, how they address existing pain points, and the benefits they bring to the organization. Change management should include training sessions, user education, and ongoing communication to keep stakeholders informed and engaged. Addressing concerns and providing support during the transition helps ensure a smooth adoption process. Change management is essential for maximizing the value of custom apps by fostering user acceptance and enthusiasm.

14. **Getting feedback and providing iterations:** After deployment, collecting feedback from users is vital for continuously improving custom apps. Feedback provides valuable insights into user satisfaction, identifies areas for enhancement, and helps address evolving needs. Establish mechanisms for users to provide feedback easily, such as feedback forms or support tickets. Analyze the feedback systematically and prioritize improvements based on user input. Continuous iteration involves implementing enhancements, updates, and new features based on user feedback and changing requirements. Iterative development ensures that custom apps remain aligned with the organization's goals and user expectations. By actively seeking and acting on feedback, organizations can enhance the long-term satisfaction and effectiveness of custom apps.

15. **Including legal considerations:** Legal considerations play a crucial role in custom app development, particularly when working within SAP's platform. Reviewing licensing agreements with SAP is essential to ensure compliance. Licensing agreements dictate how SAP software can be used, modified, and distributed. Non-compliance with licensing terms can result in legal issues, including penalties and interruptions in service. Therefore, it's imperative to understand and adhere to the licensing agreements relevant to custom app development. Legal compliance also extends to data privacy regulations, intellectual property rights, and contractual obligations. Ensuring adherence to legal

17

requirements protects both the organization and its stakeholders. Legal considerations are an integral part of the custom app development process, providing a solid legal foundation for the project's success.

In conclusion, the growing need for mobile applications in SAP ERP solutions reflects the dynamic nature of today's business landscape. These applications empower organizations to capitalize on real-time data, streamline operations, and engage users more effectively. However, the successful implementation of mobile ERP solutions requires careful consideration of security, integration, user training, customization, cost, and device compatibility. When executed thoughtfully, mobile applications can unlock the full potential of SAP ERP systems and drive organizations toward greater efficiency and competitiveness in a rapidly evolving world.

# CHAPTER 2

# Overview of SAP Supply Chain Processes

It is important to understand the basic supply chain processes, like purchase orders, Goods Receipts, Goods Issues, and Transfer Postings, as these will be the processes that you'll transform to iOS apps.

## The Purchase Order and Goods Receipt Processes

The SAP purchase order and goods receipt processes are critical parts of any organization's supply chain. They ensure that goods are ordered from the correct suppliers at the correct time and that they are received and inspected properly. The purchase order process begins when a buyer creates a purchase order in SAP. The purchase order specifies the material to be ordered, the quantity, the price, and the delivery date. The buyer then sends the purchase order to the supplier. Once the supplier has received the purchase order, they begin to prepare the goods for delivery.

© Pranay Gupta 2024
P. Gupta, *Digital Transformation of SAP Supply Chain Processes*,
https://doi.org/10.1007/979-8-8688-0270-6_2

When the goods are ready, the supplier creates a delivery note and sends it to the buyer. A *delivery note* is a document that lists the goods that are being delivered and the quantity of each item. The buyer uses the delivery note to check the goods when they are received. When the goods are received, the buyer creates a Goods Receipt in SAP. The *Goods Receipt* is a document that records the receipt of the goods and updates the inventory system.

The Goods Receipt process can be completed manually or automatically. When the Goods Receipt process is completed manually, the buyer enters the data from the delivery note into SAP. When the Goods Receipt process is completed automatically, SAP generates a Goods Receipt based on the data from the delivery note.

## Serialized Items

*Serialized items* are items that are uniquely identified by their serial numbers. Serialized items can be anything from electronic devices to medical devices to aircraft parts. Managing serialized items can be challenging, as each item must be tracked individually. SAP can help organizations manage serialized items by automating the purchase order and goods receipt process.

# Replacing the Insufficient Desktop-Based Goods Receipt Process with a Mobile App-Based Process

The current process involves users generating purchase orders for materials from vendors. However, upon delivery of these materials via various means (such as trucks), users manually document the Goods Receipt on paper before entering the data into the electronic system. This manual and time-consuming process warrants optimization.

With the new process, the Mobile app can scan the purchase order number using the barcode and present all the details from the purchase orders. The buyer's PO number is sent as a barcode in PO output form or suppliers can convert the PO number to a barcode when they send the bill of lading or another legal document with delivery. Users can receive the delivered quantities on each item from the vendors. This process saves time, as users can create real-time receipts right at the unloading point and can also print Goods Receipt labels and put those stickers on boxes before putting them into the staging area or into bins or racks in the warehouse. See Figure 2-1.

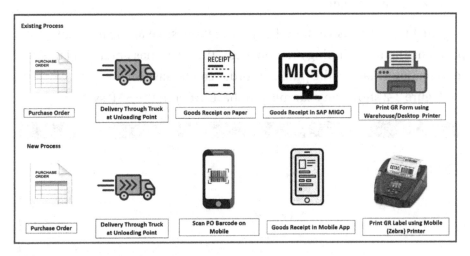

***Figure 2-1.*** *Existing desktop process vs the new Mobile app-based process*

# Creating a Purchase Order

To create a purchase order in SAP, the buyer uses the transaction code **ME21N**. The buyer enters the following information:

- Supplier

- Material

- Quantity

- Price

- Delivery date

The buyer can also enter other information, such as the terms of payment and the shipping method. Once the buyer has entered all the required information, the purchase order can be saved.

Figure 2-2 shows an example purchase order in the SAP system.

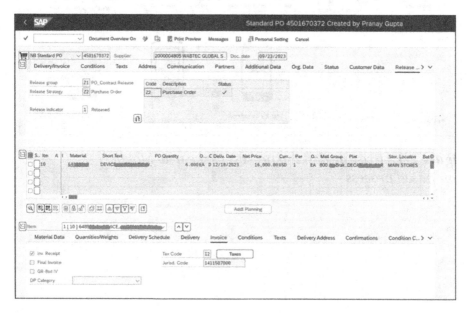

**Figure 2-2.**  *Purchase order in SAP – ME23N*

# Creating a Goods Receipt

When the goods are received, the buyer creates a Goods Receipt in SAP. To create a Goods Receipt, the buyer uses the transaction code **MIGO**. The buyer enters the following information:

- Purchase order number

- Quantity

The buyer can also enter information, such as the date of receipt and the inspection results. Once the buyer has entered all the required information, the Goods Receipt can be posted.

When the serialized items are received, the buyer will enter the serial number of all the quantities.

An example of serialized items are laptops, phones, and other electronic devices. All these devices contain IMEI codes, which are unique serial numbers. For example, say a department wants to receive 50 laptops from a company. The buyer will create a PO for 50 laptops and, when they receive the laptops, the buyer will enter the IMEI number or other unique identifiable number as the serial number so that these laptops can be identified individually in inventory.

Figure 2-3 shows how to create the Goods Receipt for the example purchase order, by entering six unique serial numbers.

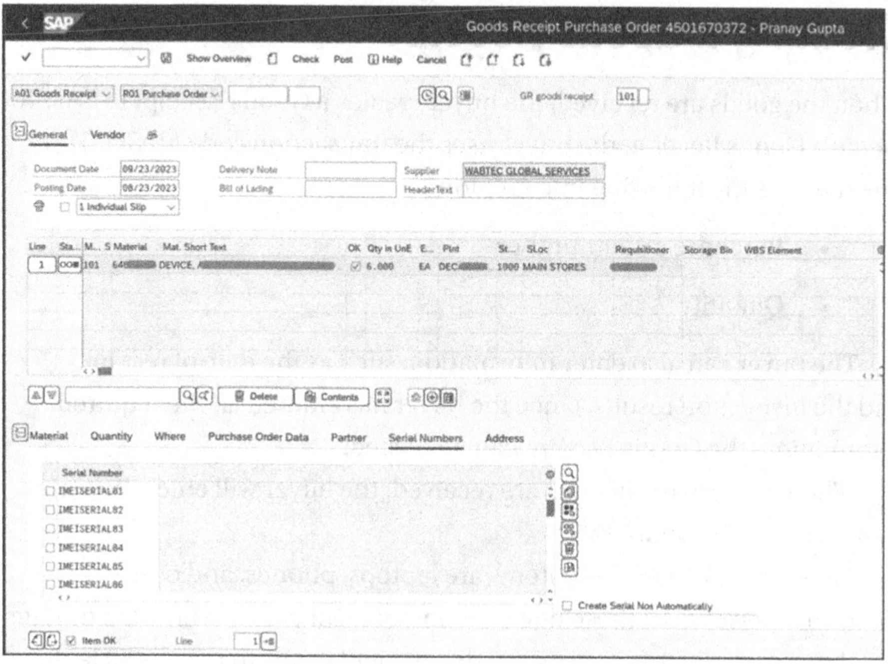

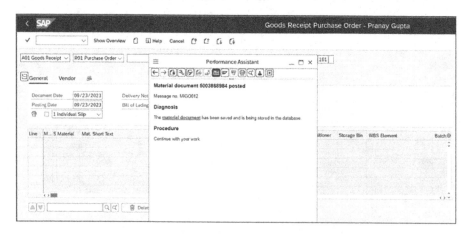

**Figure 2-3.**  *Creating a Goods Receipt - MIGO*

You can also choose to create serial numbers automatically. You can define different rules to create serial numbers for different materials, as shown in Figure 2-4.

**Figure 2-4.**  *Goods Receipt document - movement type 101*

The Goods Receipt has been posted successfully.

There are several benefits to using SAP to manage serialized items. These benefits include:

- **Improved accuracy:** Improves the accuracy of the purchase order and Goods Receipt process for serialized items by automating manual tasks.

- **Increased efficiency:** Increases the efficiency of the purchase order and Goods Receipt process for serialized items by streamlining the process and reducing the amount of time it takes to complete.

- **Improved visibility:** Provides visibility into the entire purchase order and Goods Receipt process for serialized items. This allows organizations to track the status of serialized items and identify potential problems early on.

- **Reduced costs:** Reduces the costs associated with the purchase order and Goods Receipt process for serialized items by automating manual tasks and streamlining the process.

# The Transfer Postings Process

The SAP Transfer Postings process is a fundamental component of inventory management within the SAP ERP system. It provides an efficient and structured method for organizations to manage the movement of goods within their supply chain. Transfer Postings allow for the relocation of materials, both within the same plant or storage location and between different plants and storage locations, while maintaining accurate inventory records. This overview provides a concise understanding of the key aspects of the SAP Transfer Postings process. SAP transaction code **MIGO** is used for Transfer Postings.

The purpose of Transfer Postings is as follows:

- **Inventory movement:** SAP Transfer Postings enable the movement of materials or goods from one location to another, such as from a warehouse to a production line or from one storage location to another.

- **Inventory accuracy:** They ensure that the inventory records accurately reflect the physical location of materials, helping prevent discrepancies and stockouts.

- **Stock valuation:** Transfer Postings impact how materials are valued in financial statements and reports.

# Types of Transfer Postings

*One-step transfers* involve direct movement of goods from the source location to the destination location, without an in-transit state. Stock will be reduced from the source location and added to the destination location in the same step.

In contrast, *two-step transfers* involve an intermediate state, often facilitated by stock transfer orders (STOs) or in-transit locations. The first step reduces the stock from the source location and puts the stock into the in-transit state in its destination location. The second step places the stock in its destination location. This approach offers more control and documentation, making it suitable for complex scenarios, such as inter-plant transfers

# Different Movement Types

SAP Transfer Postings are categorized into different movement types, each representing a specific type of material movement. Movement types determine the nature of the transaction, including whether it's a Goods Receipt, Goods Issue, Transfer Posting, or other inventory movement. Common movement types include 101 (Goods Receipt), 201 (Goods Issue), 301 (Transfer Posting Plant to Plant), and many more, each with its unique purpose and implication.

Let's explore some of the stock movement types in SAP—301, 303, 305, 311, 313, and 315—in order to understand their specific purposes and applications.

# Movement Type 301

This is a one-step transfer of stock from one plant to another plant. It is used when the stock is being transferred directly from the issuing plant to the receiving plant, without any intermediate storage. Movement type 301 has a value impact, meaning that the value of the stock is transferred from the issuing plant to the receiving plant at the moving average price of the issuing plant.

For example, to perform a Transfer Posting of two quantities using one-step transfer movement type 301:

| From Plant | From Sloc | To Plant | To Sloc |
|---|---|---|---|
| C423 | 1000 | C102 | 1000 |

First check the stock in plant C423-1000 and C102-1000 using the *t-code* (transaction code) **MMBE**. The results are shown in Figures 2-5 through 2-7.

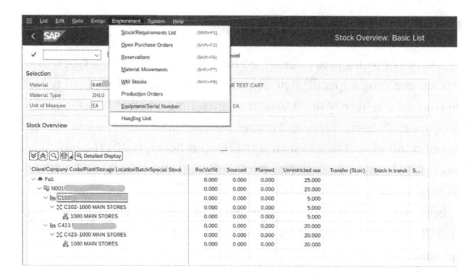

*Figure 2-5.* *Stock report - MMBE*

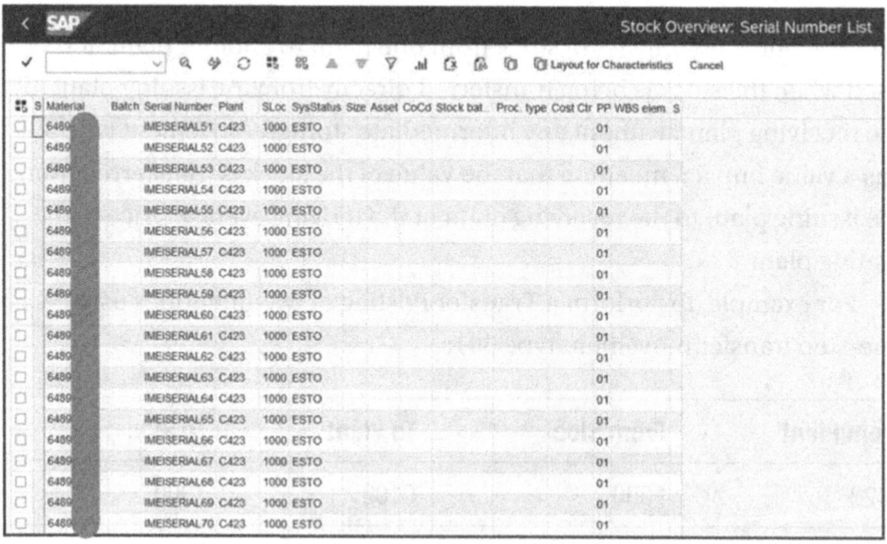

*Figure 2-6.* *Stock in plant C423 before Transfer Posting*

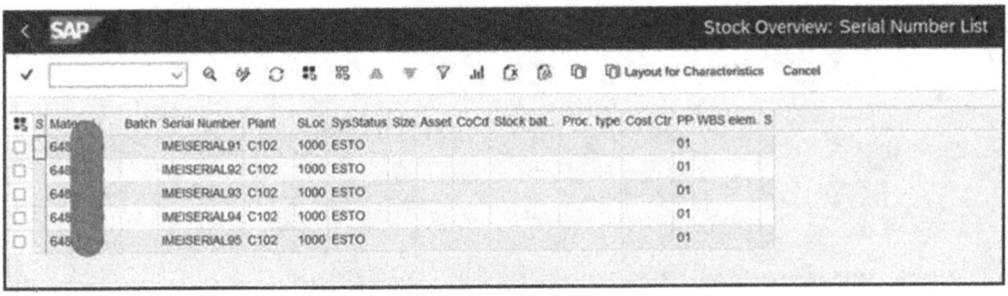

*Figure 2-7.*  *Stock in plant C102 before Transfer Posting*

Transfer two serial numbers—IMEISERIAL51 and IMEISERIAL52—from plant C423 to plant C102 using one-step transfer. See Figures 2-8 and 2-9.

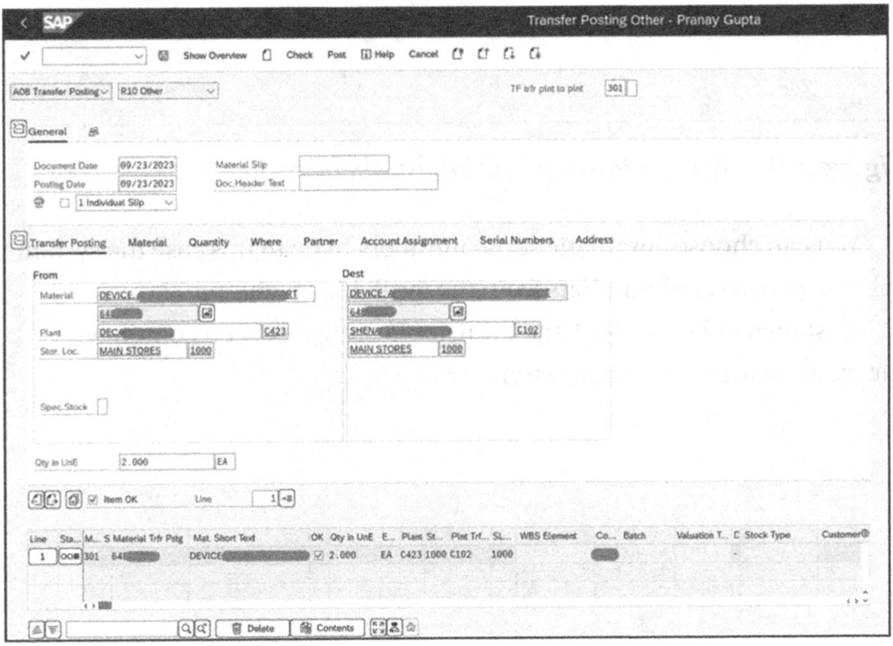

*Figure 2-8.*  *Transfer Posting - Movement Type 301 - MIGO*

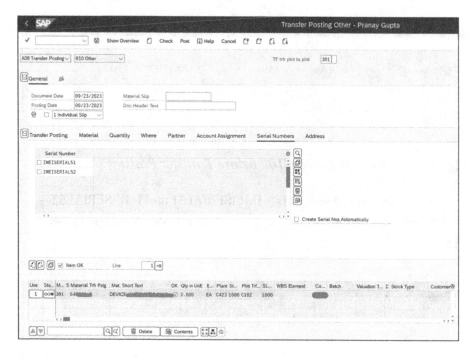

**Figure 2-9.** *Transfer Posting - serial numbers*

You can choose automatic serial numbers here; in this case the system will assign two serial numbers from the available inventory.

As shown in Figure 2-10, the Transfer Posting has been completed successfully with the one-step transfer.

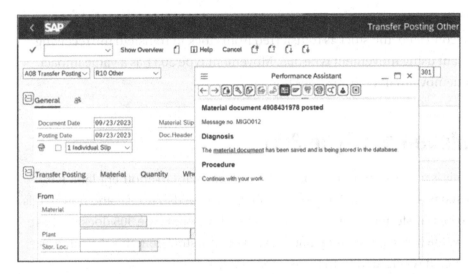

***Figure 2-10.*** *Transfer Posting Document - Movement Type 301*

You can now see the transferred serial numbers using t-code **MMBE** in plant's C102-1000 inventory, as shown in Figure 2-11.

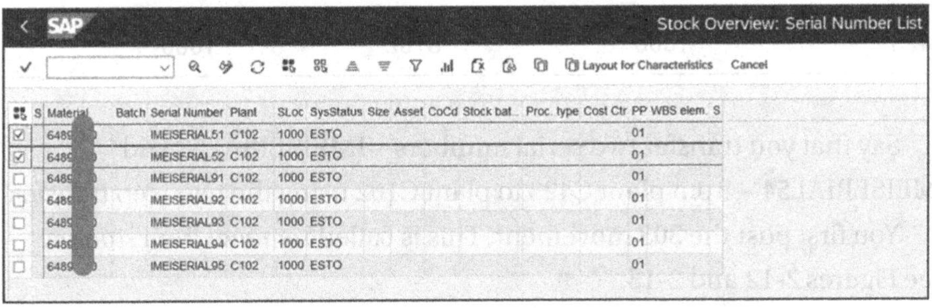

***Figure 2-11.*** *Stock in plant C102 after Transfer Posting*

# Movement Type 303

This is a two-step transfer of stock from one plant to another plant. It is used when the stock needs to be temporarily stored in transit before it is transferred to the receiving plant. In the first step, the stock is issued from the issuing plant to stock in transit using movement type 303. In the second step, the stock is transferred from stock in transit to the receiving plant using movement type 305. Movement type 303 has a value impact, but movement type 305 does not.

# Movement Type 305

This is a two-step transfer of stock from one plant to another plant. It is used when the stock has been temporarily stored in transit and now needs to be transferred to the receiving plant. Movement type 305 does not have a value impact, meaning that the value of the stock remains the same as when it was issued from the issuing plant.

For example, you can perform a Transfer Posting of two items using the two-step transfer movement types 303 and 305:

| From Plant | From Sloc | To Plant | To Sloc |
|------------|-----------|----------|---------|
| C423 | 1000 | C102 | 1000 |

Say that you transfer two serial numbers—IMEISERIAL53 and IMEISERIAL54—from plant C423 to plant C102 using the two-step transfer.

You first post the 303 movement. This is called *removal from storage*. See Figures 2-12 and 2-13.

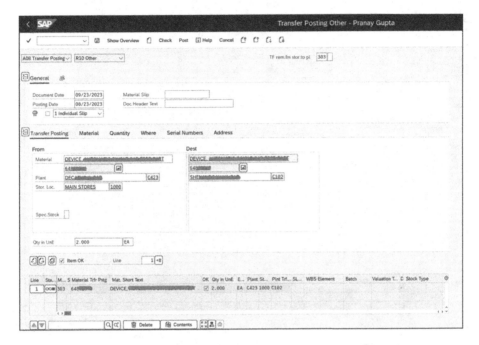

**Figure 2-12.** *Transfer Posting - movement type 303 - first step*

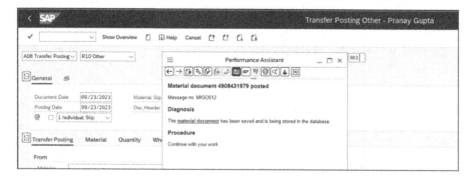

***Figure 2-13.*** *Transfer Posting - serial numbers*

As you can see in Figure 2-14, material document 4908431979 has been posted.

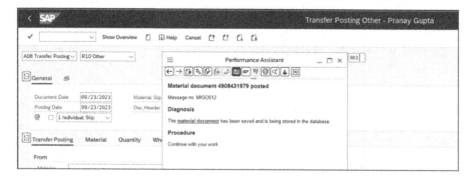

***Figure 2-14.*** *Transfer Posting document - movement type 303*

Now you can see (by using **MMBE**) that these two serial numbers have been removed from unrestricted stock in plant C423; they appear as in transit to C102. See Figure 2-15.

| S | Material | Batch | Serial Number | Plant | SLoc | SysStatus | Size | Asset | CoCd | Stock bat... | Proc. type | Cost Ctr | PP | WBS elem. | S |
|---|---|---|---|---|---|---|---|---|---|---|---|---|---|---|---|
| ☐ | 648 | | IMEISERIAL51 | C102 | 1000 | ESTO | | | | | | | 01 | | |
| ☐ | 648 | | IMEISERIAL52 | C102 | 1000 | ESTO | | | | | | | 01 | | |
| ☑ | 648 | | IMEISERIAL53 | C102 | | ESTO | | | | | | | 05 | | |
| ☑ | 648 | | IMEISERIAL54 | C102 | | ESTO | | | | | | | 05 | | |
| ☐ | 648 | | IMEISERIAL91 | C102 | 1000 | ESTO | | | | | | | 01 | | |
| ☐ | 648 | | IMEISERIAL92 | C102 | 1000 | ESTO | | | | | | | 01 | | |
| ☐ | 648 | | IMEISERIAL93 | C102 | 1000 | ESTO | | | | | | | 01 | | |
| ☐ | 648 | | IMEISERIAL94 | C102 | 1000 | ESTO | | | | | | | 01 | | |
| ☐ | 648 | | IMEISERIAL95 | C102 | 1000 | ESTO | | | | | | | 01 | | |

***Figure 2-15.*** *Stock in plant C102 before Transfer Posting - in transit status*

Now you use the 305 movement type using the earlier document that was posted using the 303 movement type. This step is called *place in storage*. During this step, you can choose the storage location where you want to place the item.

The example scenario places the items in plant C102 and store 1000, as shown in Figure 2-16.

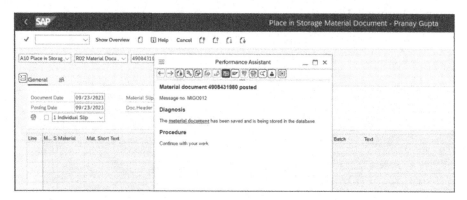

**Figure 2-16.**  *Transfer Posting - movement type 305 - second step*

As shown in Figure 2-17, 305 movement type, document 4908431980 has been posted. Now check the **MMBE** stock (see Figure 2-18).

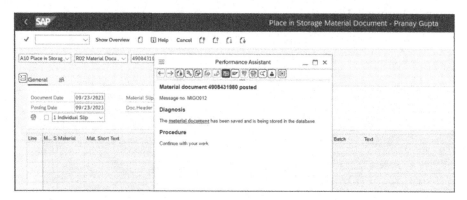

**Figure 2-17.**  *Transfer Posting document - movement type 305*

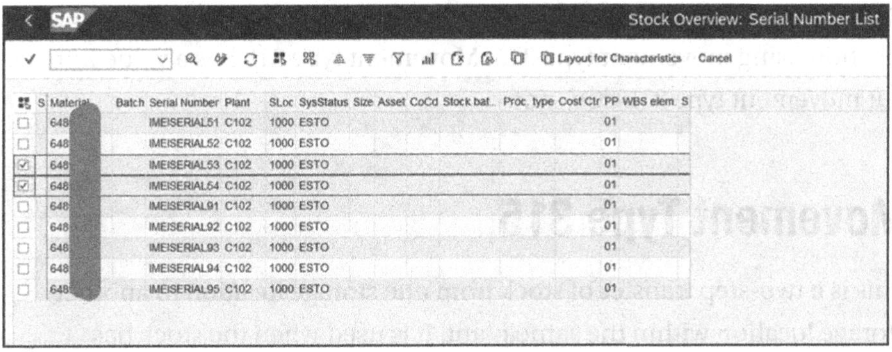

*Figure 2-18.* *The stock in plant C102 after Transfer Posting - unrestricted status*

Both serial numbers are available to use from plant C102 and store 1000.

# Movement Type 311

This is a one-step transfer of stock from one storage location to another storage location within the same plant. It is used when the stock is being moved from one area of the plant to another, such as from the warehouse to the production floor. Movement type 311 has a value impact, meaning that the value of the stock is transferred from the issuing storage location to the receiving storage location.

# Movement Type 313

This is a two-step transfer of stock from one storage location to another storage location within the same plant. It is used when the stock needs to be temporarily stored in transit before it is transferred to the receiving storage location. In the first step, the stock is issued from the issuing storage location to stock in transit using movement type 313. In the second step, the stock is transferred from stock in transit to the receiving storage location using movement type 315. Movement type 313 has a value impact, but movement type 315 does not.

# Movement Type 315

This is a two-step transfer of stock from one storage location to another storage location within the same plant. It is used when the stock has been temporarily stored in transit and now needs to be transferred to the receiving storage location. Movement type 315 does not have a value impact, meaning that the value of the stock remains the same as when it was issued from the issuing storage location.

# The Goods Issue Process

The Goods Issue process in SAP involves the movement of materials from stock to consumption, and the allocation of these goods to cost centers and work breakdown structures (WBS) is crucial for proper cost tracking. This section explains the high-level details of the SAP Goods Issue process with a focus on cost center and WBS. The process typically begins with the Goods Issue transaction (**MIGO**) in SAP. Users enter relevant information such as material number, quantity, plant, and storage location to initiate the Goods Issue.

## Cost Center Assignment

During the Goods Issue process, users can assign the consumption of materials to specific cost centers. Cost centers represent organizational units for which costs are incurred.

## WBS Element Assignment

Similarly, users have the option to allocate the Goods Issue to specific
Work Breakdown Structures (WBS elements). WBS elements are part of
project management in SAP and are used to track costs and resources at a
more granular level within projects.

# Creating a Goods Issue with Cost Center Consumption

As an example, let's check the stock in plant C102 for material, based on
the previous example. See Figure 2-19.

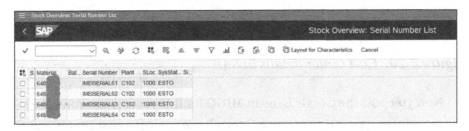

***Figure 2-19.*** *Stock in plant C102 before Cost Center Consumption*

Say you create a Goods Issue for two serial numbers—IMEISERIAL61
and IMEISERIAL62—to Cost Center 60302.

You can check the Cost Center details using the t-code **KS03**. See
Figure 2-20.

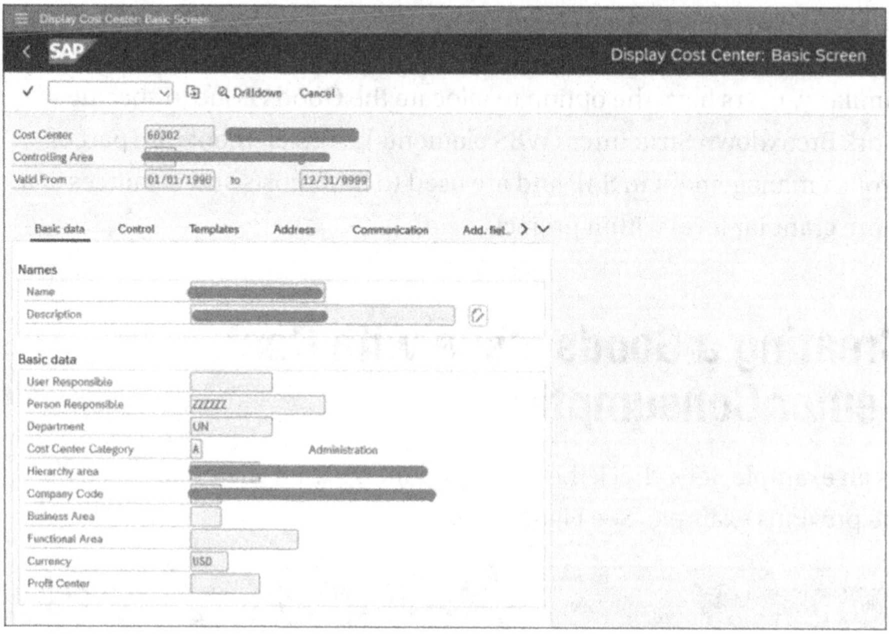

***Figure 2-20.*** *Cost center details in SAP*

Now you post the Goods Issue in **MIGO** for this cost center. You have to use movement type 201 to create a Goods Issue against a cost center. See Figures 2-21 and 2-22.

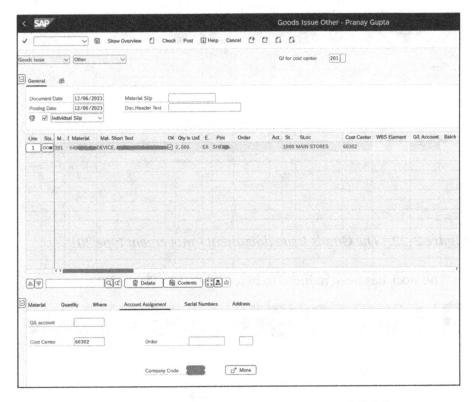

***Figure 2-21.*** *Create a Goods Issue on a cost center- MIGO*

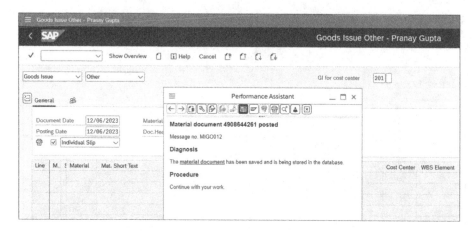

**Figure 2-22.**  *The Goods Issue document - movement type 201*

The stock has been reduced to two, as shown in Figure 2-23.

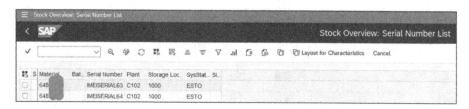

**Figure 2-23.**  *Stock in plant C102 after the Cost Center consumption*

# Creating a Goods Issue with WBS Consumption

In this example, you create a Goods Issue for two serial numbers—
IMEISERIAL63 and IMEISERIAL64—to WBS 250846-17-1

You can check the WBS details using the t-code **CJ20N**, as shown in
Figure 2-24.

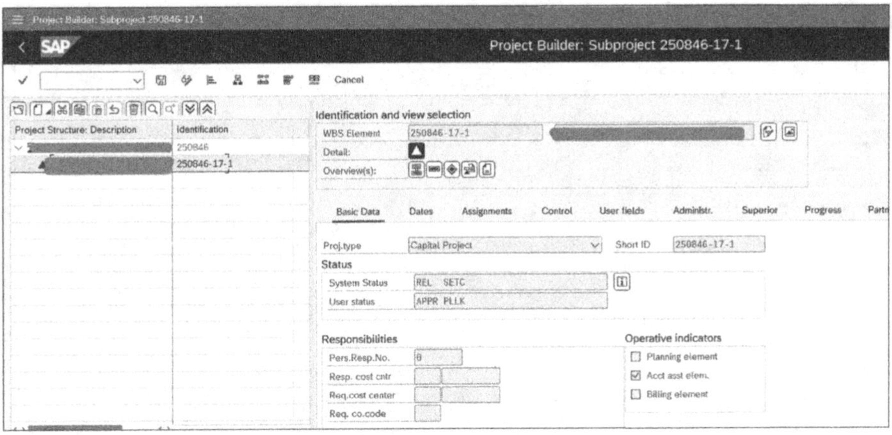

***Figure 2-24.*** *WBS element details in SAP*

Now post the Goods Issue in **MIGO** for this WBS 250846-17-1. You have to use movement type 221 to post a Goods Issue against a WBS. See Figures 2-25 through 2-27.

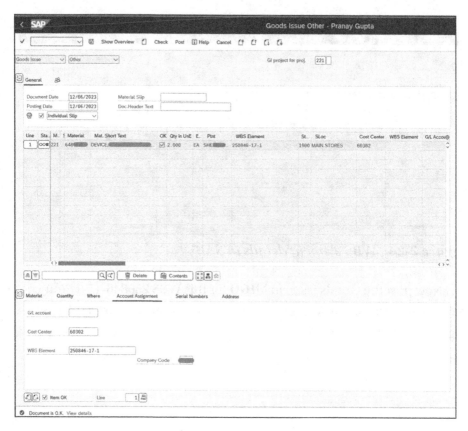

***Figure 2-25.*** *Create a Goods Issue on a WBS element - MIGO*

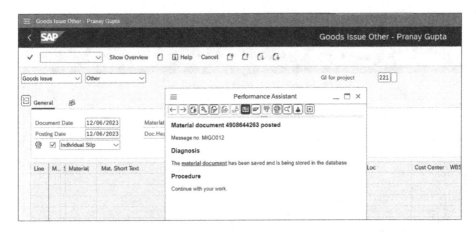

*Figure 2-26.* *Goods Issue document - Movement Type 221*

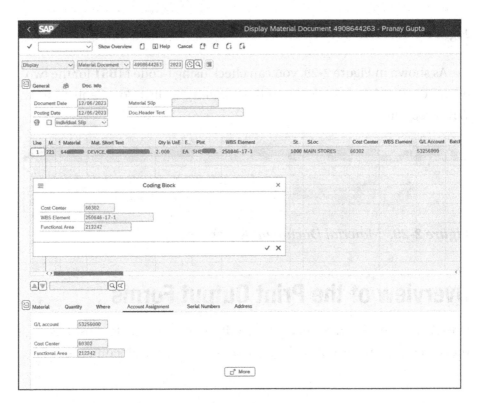

*Figure 2-27.* *Goods Issue document - account assignment details*

The stock has been reduced to 0, as shown in Figure 2-28.

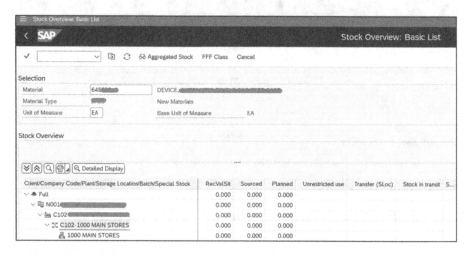

***Figure 2-28.***  *The stock in plant C102 after WBS consumption*

As shown in Figure 2-29, you can check using t-code **MB51** for the two documents, which show consumption quantity against Cost Center and WBS accordingly.

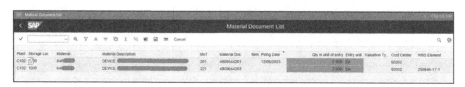

***Figure 2-29.***  *Material Document Report - MB51*

# Overview of the Print Output Forms

Now that you have a grasp of the Goods Receipt and Transfer Postings processes, it's time to look at the print outputs for these documents.

# The Goods Receipt Form

As you have learned, the Goods Receipt form is a critical document used to record and acknowledge the receipt of goods or materials into an organization's inventory. It serves as a formal acknowledgment of the delivery of goods from a supplier or an internal source. This form is essential for maintaining accurate inventory records, ensuring accountability in the supply chain, and facilitating various financial and procurement processes.

The following key information is included in a Goods Receipt form:

- **Header information:** This section typically includes details such as the company's name, address, supplier information (if applicable), purchase order number, and the date of the goods receipt.

- **Material details:** An itemized list of the received materials, including descriptions, part numbers, quantities, and units of measure. This section provides a clear breakdown of what was received.

- **Quality inspection results:** If quality control procedures are in place, the form may include information regarding inspections, acceptance status, and any deviations or issues found during the inspection.

- **Authorized signatures:** There is usually space for authorized personnel to sign or approve the Goods Receipt, confirming that the materials were received in the expected condition and quantity.

# The Transfer Posting Form

As you have learned, the Transfer Posting form is used to document and authorize the movement of materials within an organization. It is a key document for internal material management, allowing for the transfer of goods between different storage locations, plant locations, or for other purposes like scrapping or adjusting inventory quantities. This form ensures proper tracking and accounting of internal material movements.

Key information on the Transfer Posting form includes:

- **Header information:** This section typically contains details such as the company's name, relevant organizational data, transfer order number, and the date of the transfer.

- **Material details:** An itemized list of the materials being transferred, specifying part numbers, descriptions, quantities, and both the source and destination storage locations.

- **Reason for transfer:** An explanation or code indicating the purpose of the transfer, such as stock relocation, quality control, consumption, or any other specific reason for the movement.

- **Authorized signatures:** Space for authorized personnel to sign or approve the transfer, therefore ensuring that it has been properly authorized and documented.

# Purpose of the Output Forms

The Goods Receipt and Transfer Posting forms serve several important purposes, including:

- **Inventory management:** Updating inventory records to reflect the new location and status of materials accurately.

- **Internal controls:** Ensuring that material movements are properly authorized and documented, thus enhancing internal control procedures.

- **Accounting and reporting:** Providing a clear record of material transfers for accounting and reporting purposes.

- **Supply chain optimization:** Facilitating the efficient flow of materials within the organization by allowing for organized and documented movements.

# Printing the Output Forms

Both the Goods Receipt and Transfer Posting forms are integral to SAP's Material Management (MM) module and are essential for organizations to maintain accurate inventory records, streamline operations, and comply with regulatory and quality control requirements.

To print an output form for a Goods Receipt or Transfer Posting transaction, you can use the transaction code **MB90**. In this transaction, users can select the type of output form that they want to print and the material document number for the transaction.

Depending on the customization settings in SAP, these forms can be printed immediately after a document is posted or can be printed later using batch jobs or different t-codes for the relevant document.

# Configuring Output Types in SAP

Configuring SAP print output for Goods Receipt involves defining the output settings and assigning them to the Goods Receipt document type. You can use standard output types available, or you can configure your own forms and output types to print the documents. In most cases, you'll need a new form that is specific to the client's company logo and includes custom fields.

Here are the steps to configure SAP print output for a Goods Receipt:

1. **Access SAP Customizing:** You need the appropriate permissions to access SAP Customizing. You can typically access it using transaction code **SPRO** or through the SAP Easy Access menu.

2. **Define the output type for the Goods Receipt:** Navigate to the following path in SAP Customizing: **SAP Customizing Implementation Guide (SPRO) ➤ Materials Management ➤ Inventory Management and Physical Inventory ➤ Output Determination ➤ Maintain Output Types.** There, you define a new output type specific to Goods Receipt (GR). If there's already an existing output type, you can adjust it as needed.

3. **Define access sequences:** Access sequences and condition tables determine when the output should be triggered and under what conditions. Configure them based on your business requirements. Navigate to the following path: **SAP Customizing Implementation Guide (SPRO) ➤ Materials Management ➤ Inventory Management and Physical Inventory ➤ Output Determination ➤**

**Maintain Access Sequences**. Then define or adjust access sequences and condition tables to match your criteria for triggering output during a Goods Receipt.

4. **Define condition tables:** Choose **SAP Customizing Implementation Guide (SPRO) ➤ Materials Management ➤ Inventory Management and Physical Inventory ➤ Output Determination ➤ Maintain Condition Tables.**

5. **Define the output determination procedure:** Choose **SAP Customizing Implementation Guide (SPRO) ➤ Materials Management ➤ Inventory Management and Physical Inventory ➤ Output Determination ➤ Maintain Output Determination Procedures.** Then create or adjust an output determination procedure that includes the output type assigned to the Goods Receipt document type. This procedure determines the sequence of conditions and accesses to be checked for output determination.

6. **Define the output channel and medium:** Ensure you have defined the appropriate output channel (e.g., print) and output medium (e.g., printer) for your output type.

7. **Test and verify:** Before finalizing the configuration, test the output settings by performing a Goods Receipt transaction in SAP. Ensure that the output is triggered correctly and sent to the designated printer.

8. **Verify user-specific settings:** Users can also specify their preferred output devices in their SAP user profiles, which can override the default settings defined in the configuration.

This example creates a custom output type for this scenario. You can configure a custom output type ZGR1, which will be triggered while posting a Goods Receipt for any purchase orders. See Figure 2-30.

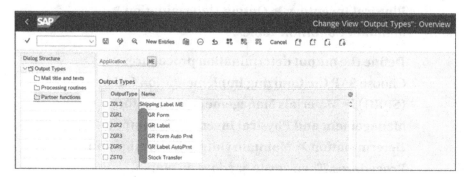

***Figure 2-30.*** *Output types assignment to a purchasing application*

ZGR1 is assigned to application ME and access sequence 003 is assigned to output type.

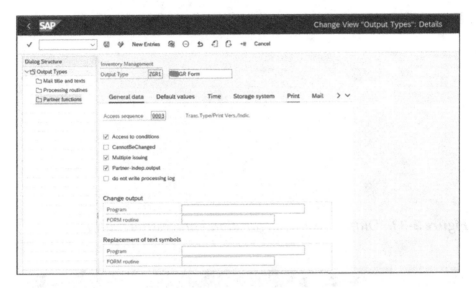

***Figure 2-31.*** *Output type configuration - general data*

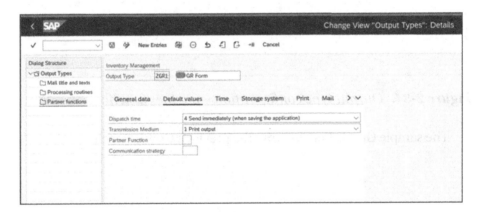

***Figure 2-32.*** *Output type configuration - default values*

The custom GR form has been attached to the custom GR output.

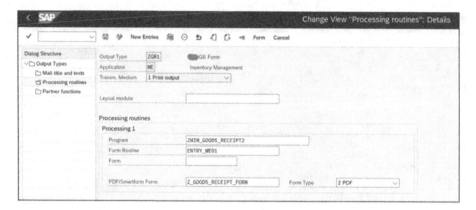

***Figure 2-33.*** *Output type configuration - processing routines*

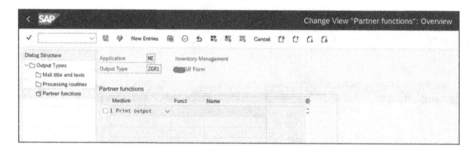

***Figure 2-34.*** *Output type configuration – partner functions*

The sample Goods Receipt from the previous Goods Receipt.

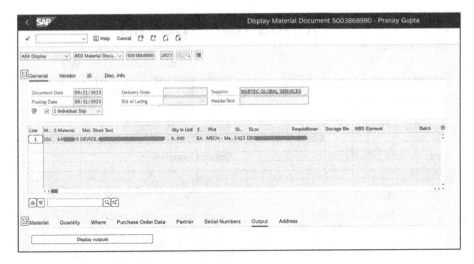

***Figure 2-35.*** *Goods Receipt document overview - MIGO*

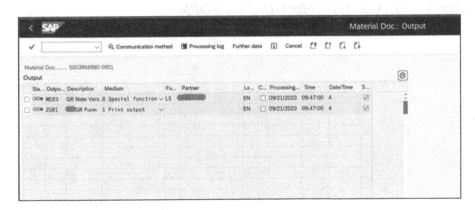

***Figure 2-36.*** *Goods Receipt output type*

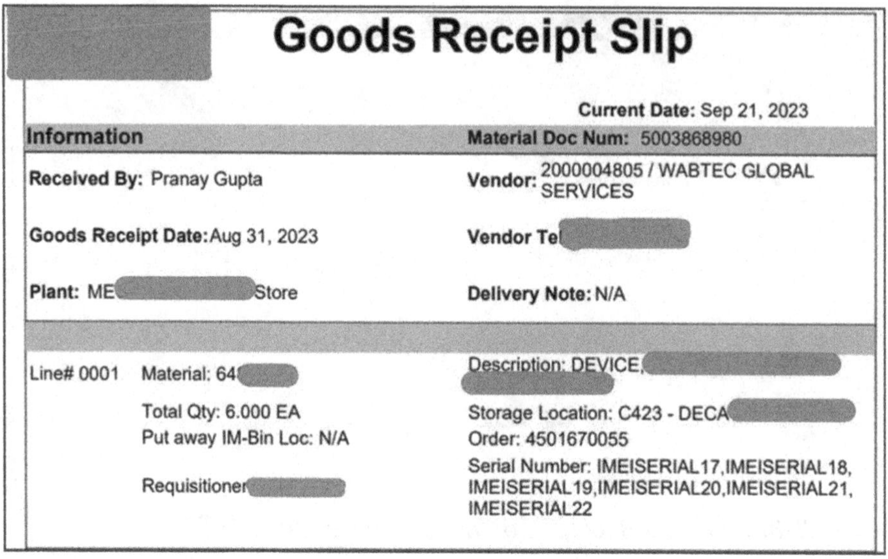

# Goods Receipt Slip

**Current Date:** Sep 21, 2023

| Information | Material Doc Num: 5003868980 |
|---|---|
| **Received By:** Pranay Gupta | **Vendor:** 2000004805 / WABTEC GLOBAL SERVICES |
| **Goods Receipt Date:** Aug 31, 2023 | **Vendor Tel** |
| **Plant:** ME[____]Store | **Delivery Note:** N/A |

Line# 0001    Material: 64[____]

  Total Qty: 6.000 EA
  Put away IM-Bin Loc: N/A

  Requisitioner[____]

**Description:** DEVICE,[____]

Storage Location: C423 - DECA[____]
Order: 4501670055
Serial Number: IMEISERIAL17,IMEISERIAL18, IMEISERIAL19,IMEISERIAL20,IMEISERIAL21, IMEISERIAL22

***Figure 2-37.*** *Goods Receipt OUTPUT FORM*

# CHAPTER 3

# Overview of OData Services

OData (Open Data Protocol) services are a set of standards for building and consuming RESTful APIs (Application Programming Interfaces) that expose data and functionality over the Internet. OData is a protocol for designing and interacting with web services in a uniform and standardized way, making it easier for developers to create and consume APIs for data access. Here are some key characteristics and aspects of OData services:

- **RESTful protocol:** OData services are based on the principles of Representational State Transfer (REST), which means they use standard HTTP methods (GET, POST, PUT, and DELETE) and adhere to RESTful architectural constraints. This makes OData services easy to understand and use.

- **Data-centric:** OData is primarily designed for exposing data, often from databases or data sources, through APIs. It allows clients to perform CRUD (Create, Read, Update, Delete) operations on data resources using HTTP methods.

© Pranay Gupta 2024
P. Gupta, *Digital Transformation of SAP Supply Chain Processes*,
https://doi.org/10.1007/979-8-8688-0270-6_3

- **Uniform resource identifier (URI):** Each data resource in an OData service is identified by a unique URI, making it accessible via a standard URL. For example, an OData URI might look like `https://example.com/OData/Products`.

- **Standardized query language:** OData provides a standardized query language that allows clients to filter, sort, and shape the data they retrieve. Queries are typically expressed using query options appended to the URI, such as `$filter`, `$orderby`, and `$select`.

- **Metadata:** OData services often include metadata that describe the structure of the data exposed by the service. This metadata can be accessed via a predefined URI, making it possible for clients to understand the data model without prior knowledge.

- **Format-agnostic:** OData supports multiple data formats, including JSON and XML, allowing clients to request data in the format that best suits their needs. JSON is a common choice due to its lightweight and human-readable nature.

- **Support for navigation:** OData services can represent relationships between data entities, allowing clients to navigate from one entity to related entities. This is achieved through navigation properties and links.

- **Security:** OData services can be secured using standard authentication and authorization mechanisms. Access to data resources can be controlled to ensure that only authorized clients can retrieve or modify data.

- **Extensibility:** OData is extensible, meaning that it can be customized to meet specific application requirements. Custom operations and functions can be added to OData services to perform complex tasks beyond basic CRUD operations.

- **Interoperability:** OData is designed to be platform-agnostic and is supported by various programming languages and frameworks. This promotes interoperability between different systems and allows for a wide range of client applications to interact with OData services.

OData services are commonly used in web and mobile applications to access and manipulate data from various sources, such as databases, cloud services, and IoT (Internet of Things) devices. They provide a standardized way to expose and consume data over HTTP, making data integration and consumption more straightforward and consistent.

# Creating an OData Service in SAP

Creating an OData service in SAP involves several steps, and the specific process may vary depending on your SAP system version and your requirements. What follows is a general guideline for creating an OData service in SAP.

# Prerequisites

Before you begin, make sure you have the necessary permissions and access to the SAP Gateway service builder (transaction code **SEGW**) and the relevant SAP system components installed. You'll also need the required data sources and entities in your SAP system.

# Create an OData Service in SAP

Follow these steps to create an OData service in SAP:

1. **Open SAP Gateway Service Builder.** Launch the SAP Gateway Service Builder by entering transaction code SEGW in the SAP GUI.

2. **Create a project.** In the SAP Gateway Service Builder, create a new project by selecting File ➤ New Project.

3. **Define the data model.** In your project, define the data model. This involves defining the entities and properties that you want to expose through the OData service. You can define these manually or import them from existing data structures in your SAP system.

4. **Define entity sets and associations.** Define entity sets that represent collections of data and associations that establish relationships between entities.

5. **Create a service implementation.** Create a service implementation for your project. This is where you define the logic for CRUD (Create, Read, Update, Delete) operations on your entities.

6. **Define the service binding.** In the service implementation, define the binding that links your entity sets and operations to the OData service.

7. **Generate runtime objects.** Generate runtime objects for your OData service. This step creates the necessary ABAP classes and artifacts for your service.

8. **Activate and maintain the service.** Activate your OData service by clicking the Activate button in the SAP Gateway Service Builder. You can also use the transaction code /n/IWFND/MAINT_SERVICE to maintain and activate your services.

9. **Test your OData service.** To test your OData service, use the built-in testing tool in the SAP Gateway Service Builder or a web-based OData client like SAP Fiori Launchpad or POSTMAN. Ensure that your service works as expected and that data can be retrieved, created, updated, and deleted.

10. **Publish your OData service.** Once you've tested and verified your OData service, you can publish it so that it's accessible to other applications and clients.

11. **Secure your OData service.** Implement security measures to protect your OData service, such as authentication and authorization. You can use SAP's security mechanisms to control access to your service.

12. **Document and monitor your service.** Document your OData service, including its entities, properties, and operations. Consider using SAP's built-in documentation tools. Additionally, set up monitoring and logging for your service to track usage and diagnose issues.

13. **Maintain and enhance your service.** Regularly maintain and enhance your OData service as needed to meet changing business requirements. You can use the SAP Gateway Service Builder to make modifications and improvements.

14. **Deploy your service.** Deploy your OData service
    to a production environment as necessary. Ensure
    that it's accessible to the intended users and
    applications.

15. **Implement versioning (optional).** Consider
    implementing versioning for your OData service to
    manage changes and ensure backward compatibility
    as you make updates and enhancements.

Note that this is a high-level overview, and the specific steps
and options may vary depending on your SAP system version and
configuration. Additionally, you may need to consult SAP documentation
and possibly involve SAP Gateway experts or developers for more complex
scenarios.

# An Example of an OData Service from a SAP System

This section contains an example of OData services that you'll use in the
app for Goods Receipt and Transfer Posting.

This example includes a custom OData service that has different entity
sets to fetch data that will be passed to the frontend for the Goods Receipt,
Transfer Posting, and Output Forms functions. See Figure 3-1.

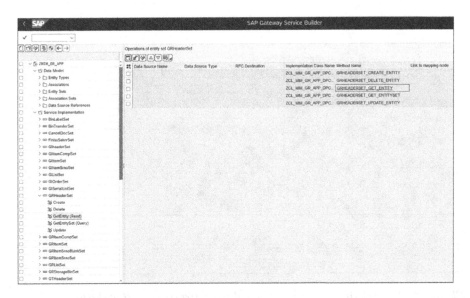

***Figure 3-1.***  *Example OData service in a SAP ECC system*

---

**Note**    This example uses the SAP ECC system and a custom OData service. In SAP S4/HANA systems, there are existing OData services that are used in standard Fiori apps.

---

You need to create entity sets that will provide data for Goods Receipt, Goods Issue, Transfer Posting, and Print functions on the Mobile app.

## Purchase Order Details Entity Set

You need to fetch the PO details that will be populated to facilitate a Goods Receipt. Figure 3-2 shows the fields that are included in this example, but you can add more fields as needed.

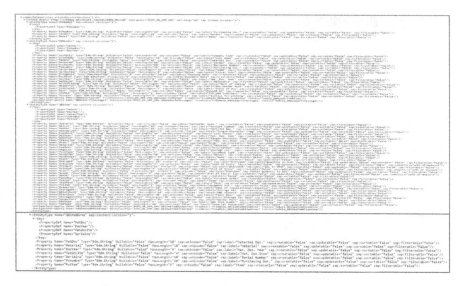

***Figure 3-2.*** *OData service entity set for purchase order details*

This example uses a nested structure so that you can populate serial numbers for each item in PO.

The structure is as follows:

- PO Header Details

- PO Item Details

- PO Item Serial Number Details

# Transfer Posting Details Entity Set

You need to capture details that will be populated to facilitate the Transfer Postings. Figure 3-3 shows the fields that are included in this example, but you can add more fields as needed.

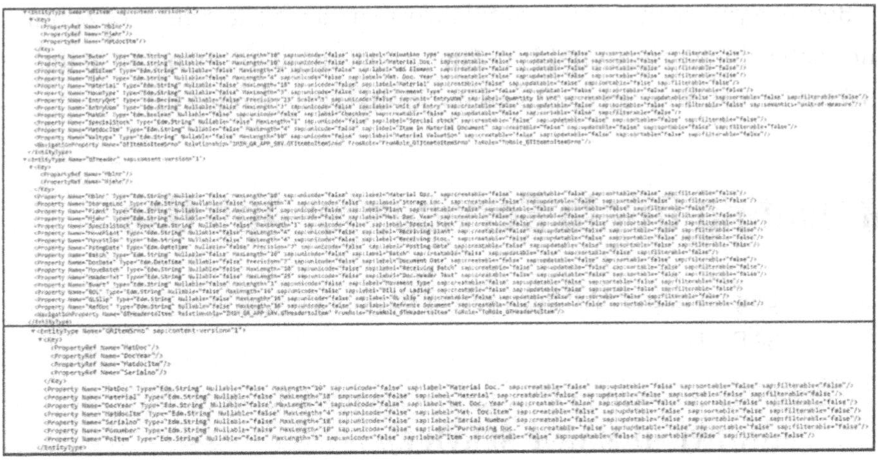

***Figure 3-3.*** *OData service entity set for Transfer Posting details*

A nested structure is used so that you can populate serial numbers for each item in Goods Transfer.

The structure is as follows:

- Goods Transfer Header Details

- Goods Transfer Item Details

- Goods Transfer Item Serial Number Details

# PDF Document Entity Set

In Chapter 2, you learned about the need for Print Output forms, which are required once documents are posted in SAP.

This example creates OData services that will transmit these PDF forms in Base64 format.

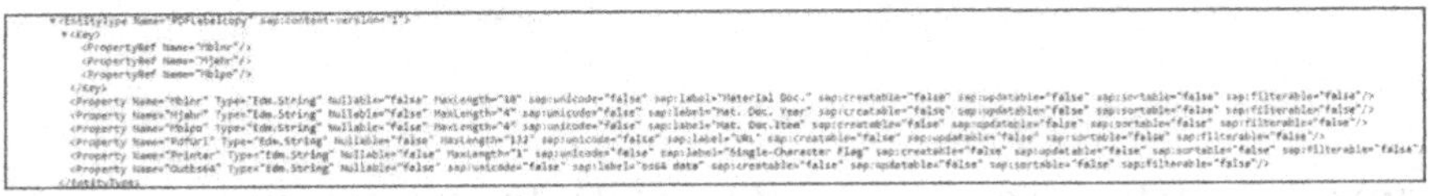

***Figure 3-4.*** *OData service entity set for a PDF form*

Because you are going to print this form on a mobile printer (a Zebra Bluetooth printer), the example creates a new output form in SAP in the 4*3 label format. You can create Adobe forms using t-code **SFP**.

# Activating OData Services for App Use

1.  Log on to the SAP Fiori server backend using SAP GUI.

2.  Enter transaction Activate and Maintain Services (**/N/IWFND/MAINT_SERVICE**).

3.  Choose Add Service.

4.  For the System Alias field, use the value Help to select the correct service. The alias should point to the SAP ECC system.

5.  Enter the service name in the Technical Service Name field and choose Enter.

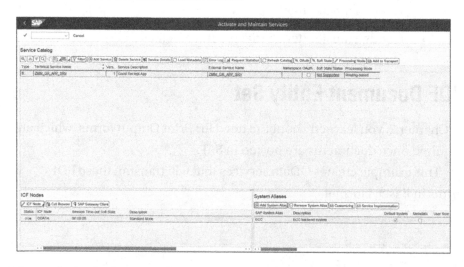

***Figure 3-5.*** *Activate and maintain an OData service using /N/IWFND/MAINT_SERVICE*

You can test the service using the Call Browser option. You can also check the error log and performance of the service using this same transaction.

You can also check error logs using t-code **/N/IWFND/ERROR_LOG**.

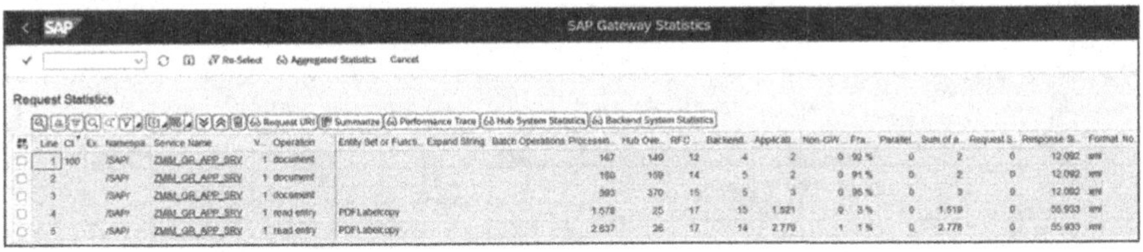

***Figure 3-6.*** *OData service performance logs using /N/IWFND/ MAINT_SERVICE*

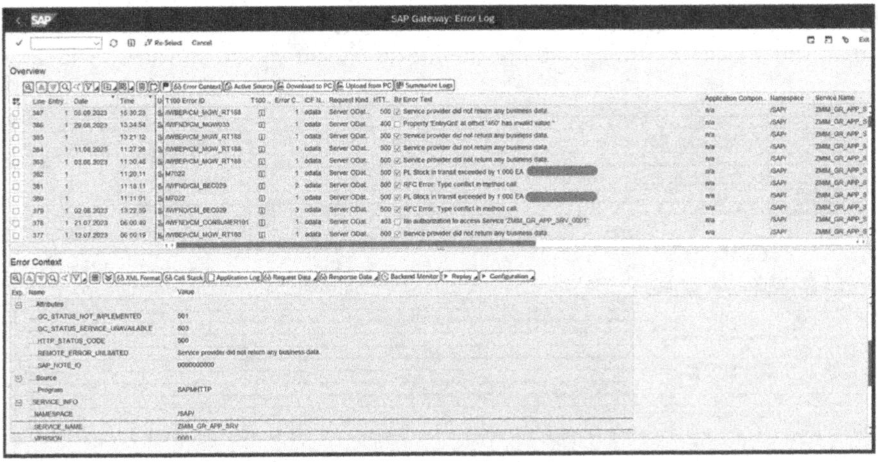

***Figure 3-7.*** *OData service error logs using /N/IWFND/ERROR_LOG*

You can also test the service using the **SICF** t-code.

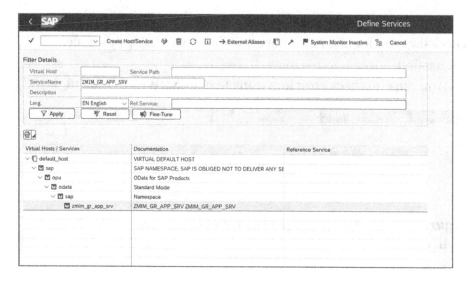

**Figure 3-8.** *Testing the OData service using SICF*

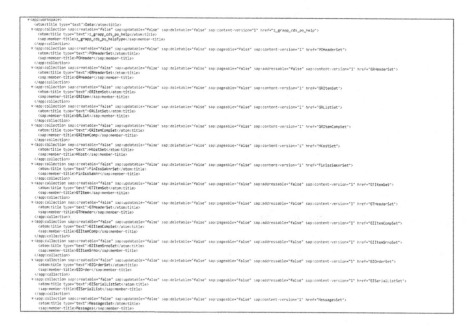

**Figure 3-9.** *OData service test results*

# JSON Messages

JSON (JavaScript Object Notation) is a lightweight data-interchange format. It is easy for humans to read and write, and it is easy for machines to parse and generate. JSON is a common data format for API responses and for storing data in files.

JSON is a text-based format that uses curly braces ({}), square brackets ([ ]), and colons (:) to represent objects and arrays. Objects are collections of key-value pairs, where the keys are strings and the values can be any valid JSON data type, such as strings, numbers, objects, arrays, or null. Arrays are ordered lists of JSON data values.

JSON can be used to represent a wide variety of data structures, such as:

- Lists of items

- Hierarchical data

- Complex objects with nested properties

# When to Use JSON

JSON is a good choice for data exchange between different systems, such as a web server and a mobile app. It is also a good choice for storing data in files, such as configuration files or log files.

# Examples of JSON Use

JSON is used in a wide variety of applications, including:

- **Web APIs:** JSON is a common format for API responses.

- **Mobile apps:** JSON is a common format for storing data on mobile devices.

69

- **Configuration files:** JSON is a common format for storing configuration files.

- **Log files:** JSON is a common format for storing log files.

- **NoSQL databases:** JSON is a common format for storing data in NoSQL databases.

# Testing OData Services as Standalone Output from a SAP Gateway System

This example tests the OData services as standalone services for your apps using the JSON format. You can test the services in **/N/WFND/ GW_CLIENT**.

## Test Service for Purchase Order Details and Goods Receipt

Figure 3-10 shows a purchase order with two serialized line items in the SAP ECC System.

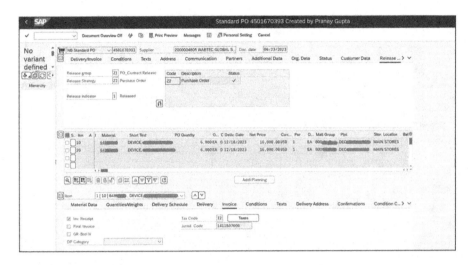

***Figure 3-10.*** *Purchase order details using ME23N*

Now you need to put the OData URL in **/N/WFND/GW_CLIENT**:

```
/sap/opu/OData/SAP/ZMIM_GR_APP_SRV/GRHeaderSet(MatDoc='',DocYear
='',PoNumber='4501670393')?$expand=GRHeadertoItem/GRItemTo
GRItemComp,GRHeadertoItem/GRItemToGRItemSrno&$format=json
```

Figure 3-11 shows the response from the OData service about the purchase order details.

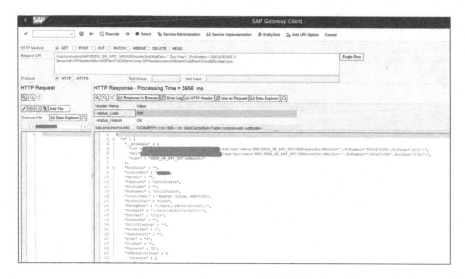

**Figure 3-11.** *Test OData service — purchase order details*

To post the Goods Receipt for this purchase order, you use this response (the Use as Request button) and fill in the quantity details and serial numbers before using the POST method.

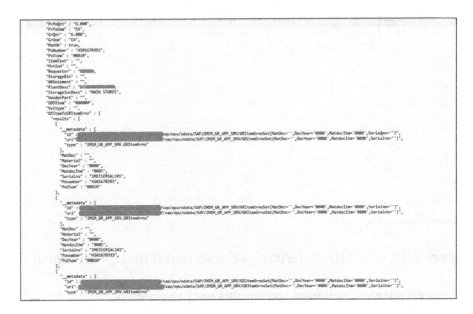

```
"PrPoQnt" : "6.000",
"PrPoUom" : "EA",
"GrQom" : "6.000",
"GrUom" : "EA",
"MatOk" : true,
"PoNumber" : "4501670393",
"PoItem" : "00010",
"ItemText" : "",
"MvtInd" : "",
"Requestor" : "        ",
"StorageBin" : "",
"WBSelement" : "",
"PlantDesc" : "DE        ",
"StoragelocDesc" : "MAIN STORES",
"VendorPart" : "",
"OBDItem" : "000000",
"ValType" : "",
"GRItemToGRItemSrno" : {
  "results" : [
    {
      "_metadata" : {
        "id" :           /sap/opu/odata/SAP/ZMIM_GR_APP_SRV/GRItemSrnoSet(MatDoc='',DocYear='0000',MatdocItm='0000',Serialno='')",
        "uri" :          /sap/opu/odata/SAP/ZMIM_GR_APP_SRV/GRItemSrnoSet(MatDoc='',DocYear='0000',MatdocItm='0000',Serialno='')",
        "type" : "ZMIM_GR_APP_SRV.GRItemSrno"
      },
      "MatDoc" : "",
      "Material" : "",
      "DocYear" : "0000",
      "MatdocItm" : "0001",
      "Serialno" : "IMEISERIAL101",
      "Ponumber" : "4501670393",
      "PoItem" : "00010"
    },
    {
      "_metadata" : {
        "id" :                    /sap/opu/odata/SAP/ZMIM_GR_APP_SRV/GRItemSrnoSet(MatDoc='',DocYear='0000',MatdocItm='0000',Serialno='')",
        "uri" :                   /sap/opu/odata/SAP/ZMIM_GR_APP_SRV/GRItemSrnoSet(MatDoc='',DocYear='0000',MatdocItm='0000',Serialno='')",
        "type" : "ZMIM_GR_APP_SRV.GRItemSrno"
      },
      "MatDoc" : "",
      "Material" : "",
      "DocYear" : "0000",
      "MatdocItm" : "0001",
      "Serialno" : "IMEISERIAL102",
      "Ponumber" : "4501670393",
      "PoItem" : "00010"
    },
    {
      "_metadata" : {
        "id" :           /sap/opu/odata/SAP/ZMIM_GR_APP_SRV/GRItemSrnoSet(MatDoc='',DocYear='0000',MatdocItm='0000',Serialno='')",
        "uri" :          /sap/opu/odata/SAP/ZMIM_GR_APP_SRV/GRItemSrnoSet(MatDoc='',DocYear='0000',MatdocItm='0000',Serialno='')",
        "type" : "ZMIM_GR_APP_SRV.GRItemSrno"
```

**Figure 3-12.**  *OData service response — purchase order details*

Table 3-1 shows that the example posts all six quantities for both items with the serial numbers.

**Table 3-1.**  *Transfer Posting Serial Numbers List*

| Item 1 Serial Number | Item 2 Serial Number |
|---|---|
| IMEISERIAL101 | IMEISERIAL107 |
| IMEISERIAL102 | IMEISERIAL108 |
| IMEISERIAL103 | IMEISERIAL109 |
| IMEISERIAL104 | IMEISERIAL110 |
| IMEISERIAL105 | IMEISERIAL111 |
| IMEISERIAL106 | IMEISERIAL112 |

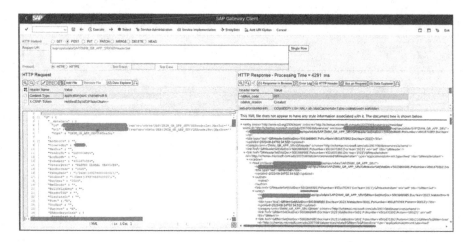

**Figure 3-13.** *Test OData service — Create Goods Receipt document*

Goods Receipt document 5003868985 has been posted.

Let's look at this document in SAP ECC.

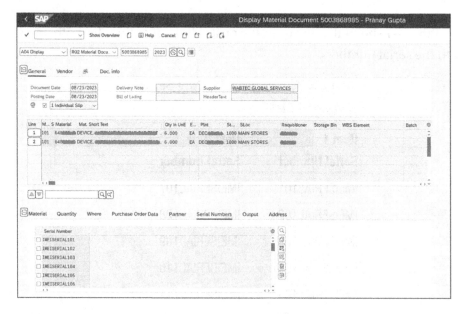

**Figure 3-14.** *Goods Receipt document details*

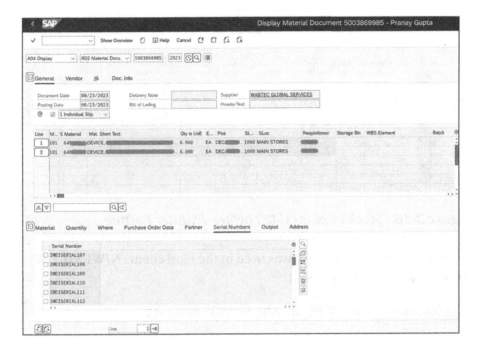

**Figure 3-15.** *Goods Receipt document — serial number details*

The Goods Receipt document has been posted successfully with all the serial numbers provided in the OData response.

Next, you'll test the Transfer Posting OData service for one-step movement type 301 and for two-step movement types 303 and 305.

# Testing the Service for Transfer Posting with One-Step Movement Type 301

This example tries to transfer two quantities of material from plant sloc C423-1000 to C102-1000 using the one-step using movement type 301.

The serial numbers IMEISERIAL59 and IMEISERIAL60 will be transferred.

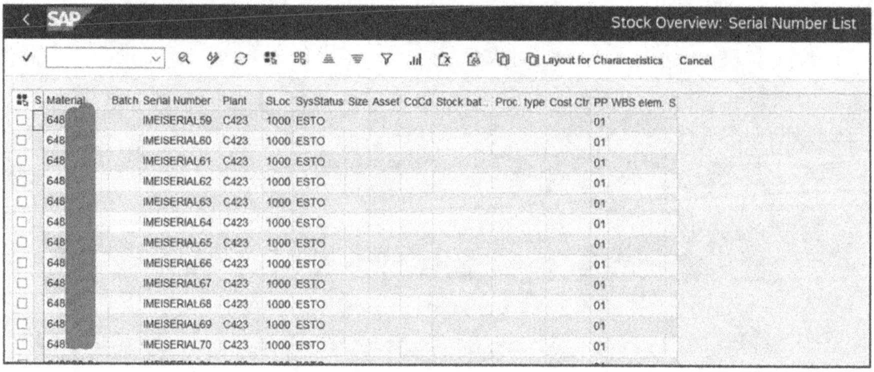

*Figure 3-16.* *Stock in plant C423 before Transfer Posting*

The following OData URL was used in the Fiori client /**N**/**WFND**/**GW_ CLIENT** with the POST method:

`/sap/opu/odata/SAP/ZMIM_GR_APP_SRV/GTHeaderSet`

*Figure 3-17.*   *Test OData service — Create Transfer Posting document - movement type 301*

Figure 3-18 shows that the request message was passed for the Transfer Posting.

```
{
  "d" : {
    "Mblnr" : "",
    "StorageLoc" : "1000",
    "Plant" : "C423",
    "Mjahr" : "",
    "SpecialStock" : "",
    "MovePlant" : "C102",
    "MoveStloc" : "1000",
    "PstngDate" : "2023-10-02T04:00:00",
    "Batch" : "",
    "DocDate" : "2023-10-02T04:00:00",
    "MoveBatch" : "",
    "HeaderTxt" : "",
    "Bwart" : "301",
    "BOL" : "",
    "GLSlip" : "",
    "RefDoc" : "",
    "GTHeadertoItem" : {
      "results" : [
        {
          "Bwtar" : "",
          "Mblnr" : "",
          "WBSElem" : "",
          "Mjahr" : "",
          "Material" : "648██████",
          "MoveType" : "301",
          "EntryQnt" : "2",
          "EntryUom" : "",
          "MatOk" : true,
          "SpecialStock" : "",
          "MatdocItm" : "0000",
          "Valtype" : "",
          "GTItemtoItemSrno" : {
            "results" : [
              {
                "Matnr" : "648██████",
                "Lgort" : "1000",
                "Werks" : "C423",
                "Serialno" : "IMEISERIAL59"
              },
              {
                "Matnr" : "648██████",
                "Lgort" : "1000",
                "Werks" : "C423",
                "Serialno" : "IMEISERIAL60"
              }
            ]
          }
        }
      ]
    }
  ]
```

*Figure 3-18.* Request JSON message for Transfer Posting - movement type 301

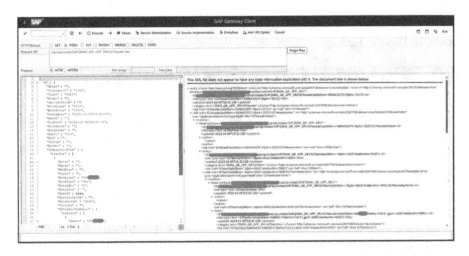

**Figure 3-19.** *Transfer Posting document - movement type 301*

Transfer Posting Document 4908432070 has been posted successfully, as shown in Figure 3-20.

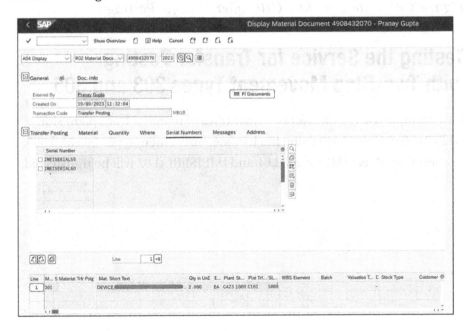

**Figure 3-20.** *Transfer Posting document overview - MIGO*

Both serial numbers were transferred successfully to C102-1000, as shown in Figure 3-21.

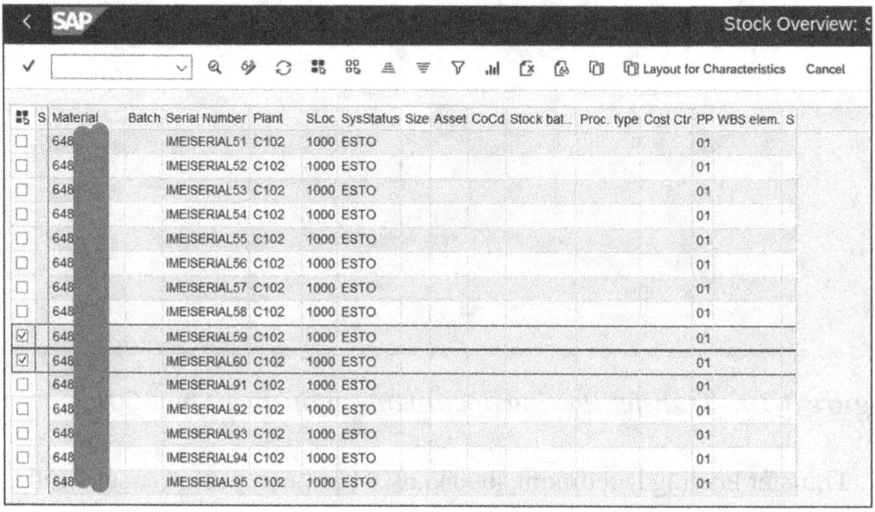

*Figure 3-21. Stock in plant C102 after Transfer Posting*

# Testing the Service for Transfer Posting with Two-Step Movement Types 303 and 305

This example tries to transfer two quantities of material from plant sloc C423-1000 to C102-1000 using the two-step movement types 303 and 305.

Serial numbers IMEISERIAL61 and IMEISERIAL62 will be transferred.

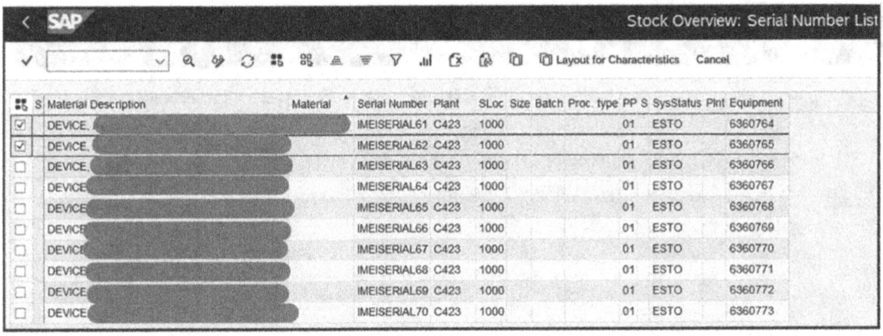

*Figure 3-22.* *Stock in plant C423 before Transfer Posting*

This transfer has two steps. The first step is to remove the stock from storage using movement type 303.

The second step is to place the stock in storage using movement type 305. The following OData URL is used in the Fiori client **/N/WFND/GW_CLIENT** with the GET method to get details about the 303 document:

```
/sap/opu/odata/sap/ZMIM_GR_APP_SRV/GTHeaderSet(Mblnr='',
Mjahr='')?$filter=(RefDoc eq '4908644092')&$expand=GTHeadertoItem,
GTHeadertoItem/GTItemtoItemSrno
```

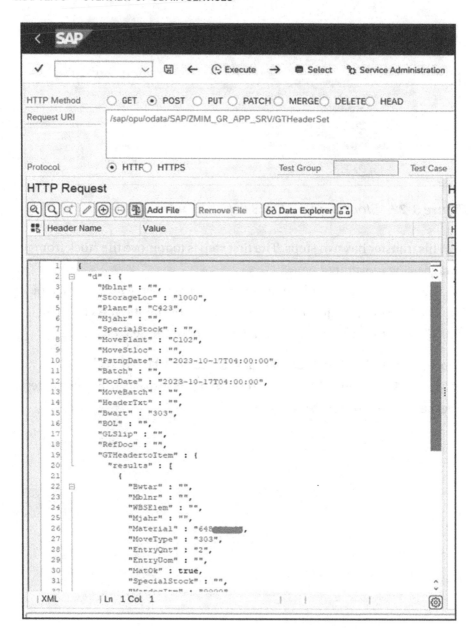

*Figure 3-23.* *Test OData service — Create Transfer Posting document - movement type 303*

As shown in Figure 3-24, the request message was passed for Transfer Posting using movement type 305.

```
{
  "d" : {
    "Mblnr" : "",
    "StorageLoc" : "1000",
    "Plant" : "C423",
    "Mjahr" : "",
    "SpecialStock" : "",
    "MovePlant" : "C102",
    "MoveStloc" : "",
    "PstngDate" : "2023-10-17T04:00:00",
    "Batch" : "",
    "DocDate" : "2023-10-17T04:00:00",
    "MoveBatch" : "",
    "HeaderTxt" : "",
    "Bwart" : "303",
    "BOL" : "",
    "GLSlip" : "",
    "RefDoc" : "",
    "GTHeadertoItem" : {
      "results" : [
        {
          "Bwtar" : "",
          "Mblnr" : "",
          "WBSElem" : "",
          "Mjahr" : "",
          "Material" : "648      ",
          "MoveType" : "303",
          "EntryQnt" : "2",
          "EntryUom" : "",
          "MatOk" : true,
          "SpecialStock" : "",
          "MatdocItm" : "0000",
          "Valtype" : "",
          "GTItemtoItemSrno" : {
            "results" : [
              {
                "Matnr" : "648      ",
                "Lgort" : "1000",
                "Werks" : "C423",
                "Serialno" : "IMEISERIAL61"
              },
              {
                "Matnr" : "648      ",
                "Lgort" : "1000",
                "Werks" : "C423",
                "Serialno" : "IMEISERIAL62"
              }
            ]
          }
        }
      ]
    }
  }
}
```

*Figure 3-24. Request JSON message for Transfer Posting — movement type 303*

Now you use the POST method to post the document.

/sap/opu/odata/SAP/ZMIM_GR_APP_SRV/GTHeaderSet

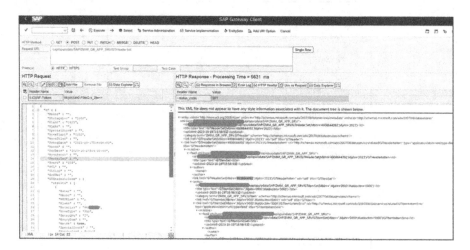

***Figure 3-25.***  *Transfer Posting document — movement type 303*

Transfer Posting document 4908644092 has been posted successfully.

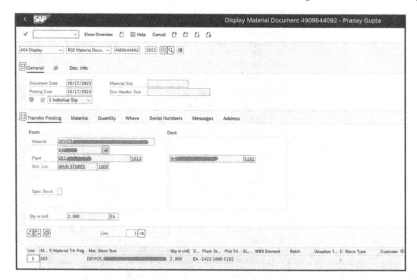

***Figure 3-26.***  *Transfer Posting document overview — movement type 303*

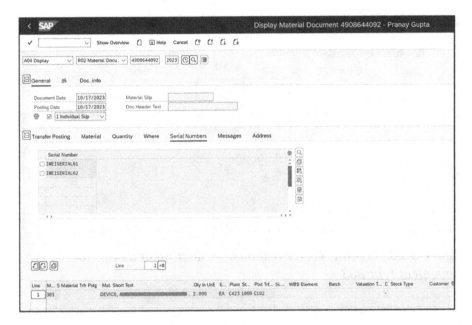

*Figure 3-27.* *Transfer Posting document — serial number details*

Now you need to perform the second step, which is to post movement type 305 to place the stock in the destination store.

This step has been incorporated into the Goods Receipt function of OData, instead of the purchase order function, so you get the details for the document posted with movement type 303 (the first step).

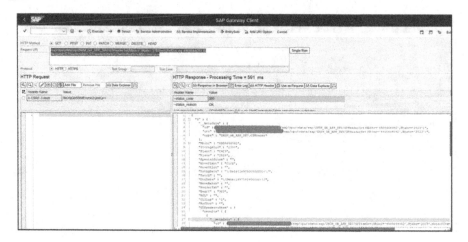

***Figure 3-28.*** *OData service response — document details for movement type 303*

*Figure 3-29.* *Test OData service — create Transfer Posting*
*document - movement type 305*

```
{
  "d" : {
    "Mblnr" : "",
    "StorageLoc" : "1000",
    "Plant" : "C102",
    "Mjahr" : "",
    "SpecialStock" : "",
    "MovePlant" : "",
    "MoveStloc" : "",
    "PstngDate" : "2023-10-17T04:00:00",
    "Batch" : "",
    "DocDate" : "2023-10-17T04:00:00",
    "MoveBatch" : "",
    "HeaderTxt" : "",
    "Bwart" : "305",
    "BOL" : "",
    "GLSlip" : "",
    "RefDoc" : "4908644092",
    "GTHeadertoItem" : {
      "results" : [
        {
          "Bwtar" : "305",
          "Mblnr" : "",
          "WBSElem" : "",
          "Mjahr" : "",
          "Material" : "648█████",
          "MoveType" : "305",
          "EntryQnt" : "2",
          "EntryUom" : "",
          "MatOk" : true,
          "SpecialStock" : "",
          "MatdocItm" : "0001",
          "Valtype" : "",
          "GTItemtoItemSrno" : {
            "results" : [
              {
                "Matnr" : "648█████",
                "Lgort" : "1000",
                "Werks" : "C102",
                "Serialno" : "IMEISERIAL61"
              },
              {
                "Matnr" : "648█████",
                "Lgort" : "1000",
                "Werks" : "C102",
                "Serialno" : "IMEISERIAL62"
              }
            ]
          }
        }
      ]
    }
  }
}
```

*Figure 3-30. Request JSON message for Transfer Posting —
movement type 305*

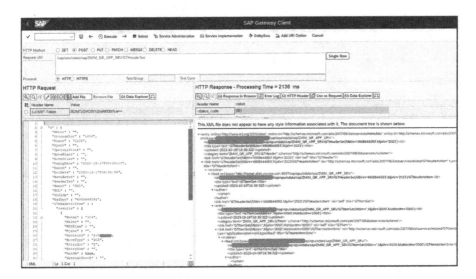

**Figure 3-31.** *Transfer Posting document — movement type 305*

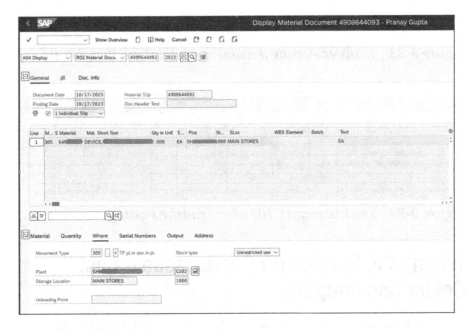

**Figure 3-32.** *Transfer Posting document overview — movement type 305*

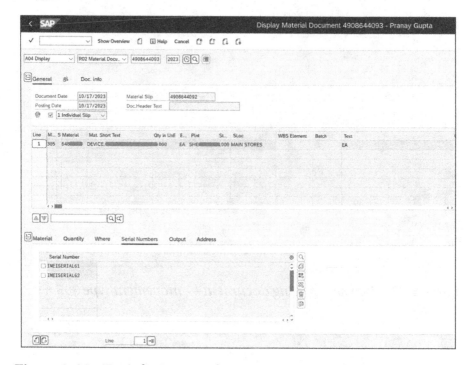

**Figure 3-33.** *Transfer Posting document — serial number details*

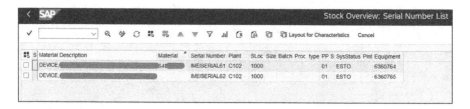

**Figure 3-34.** *Stock in plant C102 after Transfer Posting*

# Testing the Service for Goods Issue – Cost Center Consumption

Figure 3-35 shows the stock in plant C423 for the material used in the previous example.

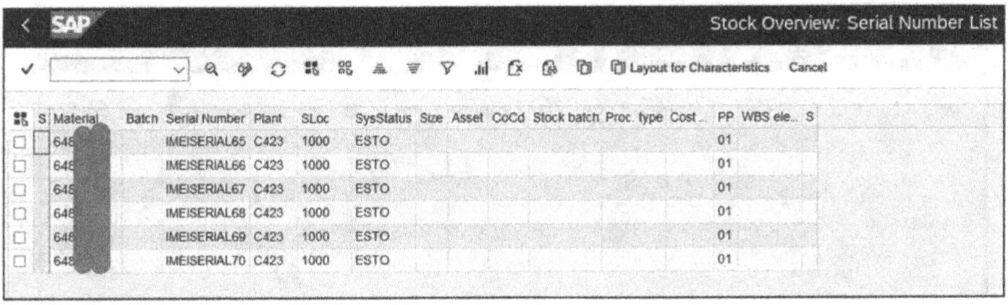

| | S | Material | Batch | Serial Number | Plant | SLoc | SysStatus | Size | Asset | CoCd | Stock batch | Proc. type | Cost | PP | WBS ele.. | S |
|---|---|---|---|---|---|---|---|---|---|---|---|---|---|---|---|---|
| ☐ | | 648 | | IMEISERIAL65 | C423 | 1000 | ESTO | | | | | | | 01 | | |
| ☐ | | 648 | | IMEISERIAL66 | C423 | 1000 | ESTO | | | | | | | 01 | | |
| ☐ | | 648 | | IMEISERIAL67 | C423 | 1000 | ESTO | | | | | | | 01 | | |
| ☐ | | 648 | | IMEISERIAL68 | C423 | 1000 | ESTO | | | | | | | 01 | | |
| ☐ | | 648 | | IMEISERIAL69 | C423 | 1000 | ESTO | | | | | | | 01 | | |
| ☐ | | 648 | | IMEISERIAL70 | C423 | 1000 | ESTO | | | | | | | 01 | | |

***Figure 3-35.*** *Stock in plant C423 before cost center Goods Issue posting*

This example creates a Goods Issue for serial numbers IMEISERIAL65 and IMEISERIAL66 to cost center 60302 using OData.

```
/sap/opu/odata/SAP/ZMIM_GR_APP_SRV/GIheaderSet
```

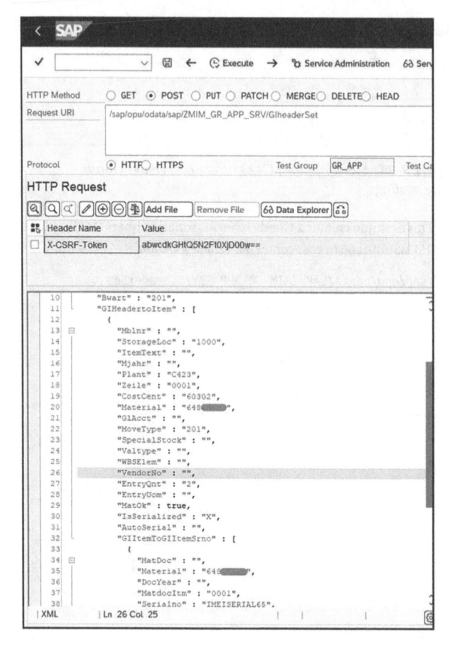

***Figure 3-36.*** *Test OData service — create a Goods Issue on cost center — movement type 201*

The request message is passed for Goods Issue posting, as shown in Figure 3-37.

```
{
  "d" : {
    "Mblnr" : "",
    "Mjahr" : "2023",
    "PstngDate" : "2023-11-17T04:00:00",
    "DocDate" : "2023-11-17T04:00:00",
    "HeaderTxt" : "",
    "OrderNo" : "",
    "OperationNo" : "",
    "Bwart" : "201",
    "GIHeadertoItem" : [
      {
        "Mblnr" : "",
        "StorageLoc" : "1000",
        "ItemText" : "",
        "Mjahr" : "",
        "Plant" : "C423",
        "Zeile" : "0001",
        "CostCent" : "60302",
        "Material" : "648▮▮▮▮",
        "GlAcct" : "",
        "MoveType" : "201",
        "SpecialStock" : "",
        "Valtype" : "",
        "WBSElem" : "",
        "VendorNo" : "",
        "EntryQnt" : "2",
        "EntryUom" : "",
        "MatOk" : true,
        "IsSerialized" : "X",
        "AutoSerial" : "",
        "GIItemToGIItemSrno" : [
          {
            "MatDoc" : "",
            "Material" : "648▮▮▮▮",
            "DocYear" : "",
            "MatdocItm" : "0001",
            "Serialno" : "IMEISERIAL65",
            "PoItem" : ""
          },
          {
            "MatDoc" : "",
            "Material" : "648▮▮▮▮",
            "DocYear" : "",
            "MatdocItm" : "0001",
            "Serialno" : "IMEISERIAL66",
            "PoItem" : ""
          }
        ]
      }
    ]
  }
}
```

*Figure 3-37.* Request JSON message for cost center Goods Issue — movement type 201

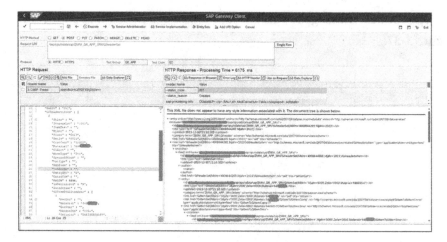

***Figure 3-38.*** *Goods Issue document — movement type 201*

Figure 3-39 shows that document 4908644265 has been posted successfully.

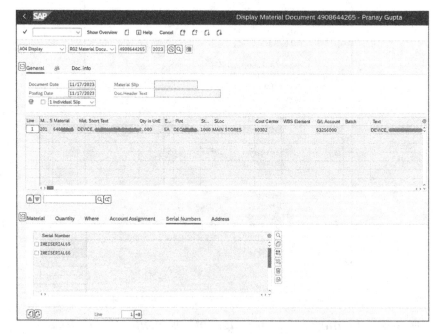

***Figure 3-39.*** *Goods Issue document overview — MIGO*

The stock has been reduced by four, as shown in Figure 3-40.

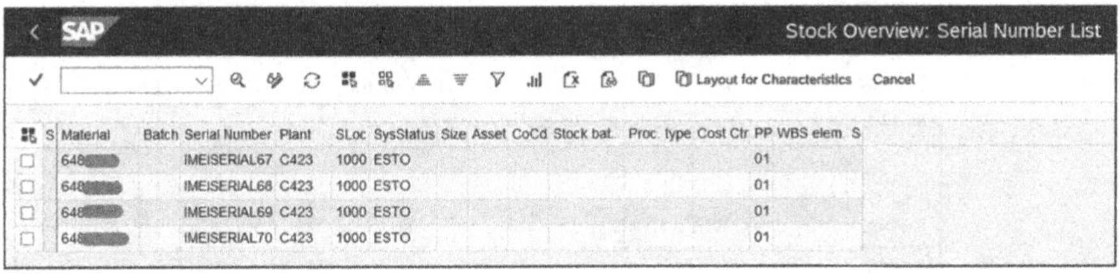

*Figure 3-40.*   *Stock in plant C423 after cost center Goods Issue posting*

# Testing the Service for Goods Issue – WBS Consumption

This example creates a Goods Issue for the serial numbers IMEISERIAL67 and IMEISERIAL68. The material is moved to WBS 250846-17-1, cost center 60302, using OData.

```
/sap/opu/odata/SAP/ZMIM_GR_APP_SRV/GIheaderSet
```

**Figure 3-41.** *Test OData service — create Goods Issue on WBS — movement type 221*

The request message is passed for Goods Issue posting, as shown in Figure 3-42.

```
{
  "d" : {
    "Mblnr" : "",
    "Mjahr" : "2023",
    "PstngDate" : "2023-11-17T04:00:00",
    "DocDate" : "2023-11-17T04:00:00",
    "HeaderTxt" : "",
    "OrderNo" : "",
    "OperationNo" : "",
    "Bwart" : "221",
    "GIHeadertoItem" : [
      {
        "Mblnr" : "",
        "StorageLoc" : "1000",
        "ItemText" : "",
        "Mjahr" : "",
        "Plant" : "C423",
        "Zeile" : "0001",
        "CostCent" : "60302",
        "Material" : "648       ",
        "GlAcct" : "",
        "MoveType" : "221",
        "SpecialStock" : "",
        "Valtype" : "",
        "WBSElem" : "250846-17-1 ",
        "VendorNo" : "",
        "EntryQnt" : "2",
        "EntryUom" : "",
        "MatOk" : true,
        "IsSerialized" : "X",
        "AutoSerial" : "",
        "GIItemToGIItemSrno" : [
          {
            "MatDoc" : "",
            "Material" : "648       ",
            "DocYear" : "",
            "MatdocItm" : "0001",
            "Serialno" : "IMEISERIAL66",
            "PoItem" : ""
          },
          {
            "MatDoc" : "",
            "Material" : "648       ",
            "DocYear" : "",
            "MatdocItm" : "0001",
            "Serialno" : "IMEISERIAL67",
            "PoItem" : ""
          }
        ]
      }
    ]
  }
}
```

*Figure 3-42.* *Request JSON message for WBS Goods Issue —*
*movement type 221*

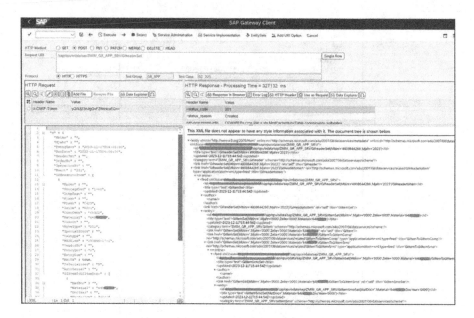

***Figure 3-43.*** *Goods Issue document — movement type 221*

Document 4908644266 has been posted successfully, as shown in Figure 3-44.

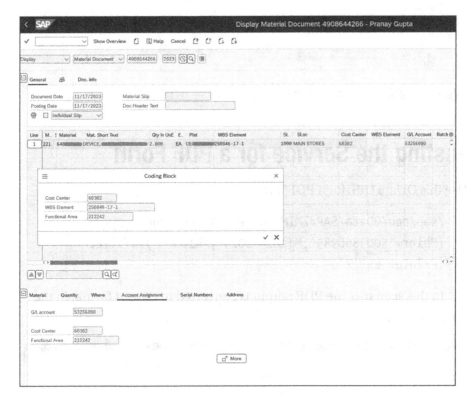

*Figure 3-44.  Goods Issue document overview — MIGO*

The stock has been reduced by two, as shown in Figure 3-45.

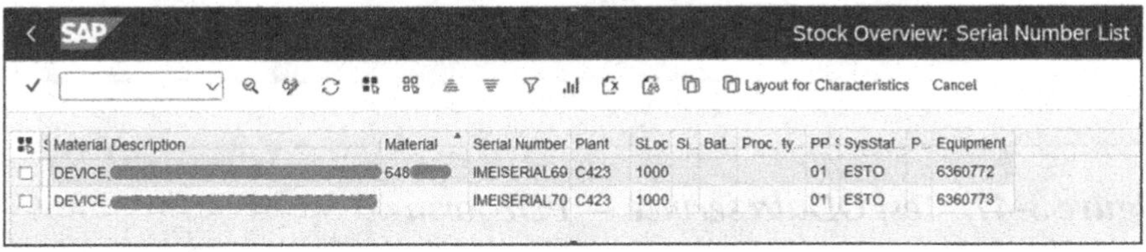

*Figure 3-45.  Stock in plant C423 after WBS Goods Issue posting*

You can check these two documents using the t-code **MB51**, which will show the consumption quantity against the cost center and WBS, accordingly. See Figure 3-46.

***Figure 3-46.*** *Material document report — MB51*

# Testing the Service for a PDF Form

Use this OData URL for a PDF form:

```
/sap/opu/OData/SAP/ZMIM_GR_APP_SRV/PDFLabelcopy
(Mblnr='5003868985',Mjahr='2023',Mblpo='')?&filter
(Printer eq 'Z')
```

In this scenario, the PDF output is converted to Base64 format in the OData service.

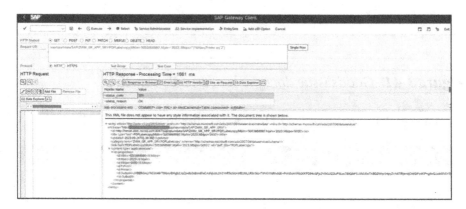

***Figure 3-47.*** *Test OData service — PDF form*

To create the PDF, this example uses an online tool that converts the output that was generated by the OData service in Base64 format to PDF format. See Figure 3-48.

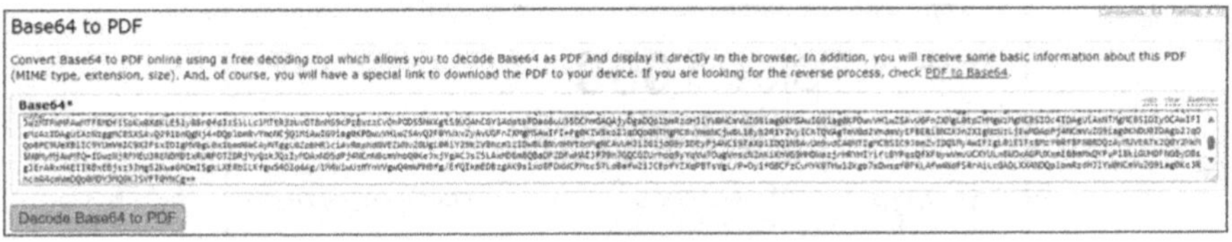

**Figure 3-48.** *Base64 to PDF conversion*

The example sends one Goods Receipt label for each serial number. Because there are six quantities for PO 4501670393 with different serial numbers, you have to send six GR labels, which are combined into one PDF containing six pages—one page for each serial number.

The labels are 4*3 so that they can be printed on a Zebra printer.

These labels are created in Adobe form using the **SFP** t-code. See Figure 3-49.

***Figure 3-49.*** *Goods Receipt PDF label*

# CHAPTER 4

# Overview of SAP BTP and SAP Mobile Services

SAP Business Technology Platform (SAP BTP) is a cloud-based platform that provides a wide range of services to help businesses innovate and grow. SAP BTP includes services for application development, integration, data management, analytics, artificial intelligence, and machine learning.

SAP Mobile Services is a set of services on SAP BTP that enables developers to build, deploy, and manage mobile apps.

## Features of SAP Mobile Services

- **Mobile app development:** SAP Mobile Services provides several tools and SDKs for developing mobile apps, including native apps, web apps, and hybrid apps.

- **Mobile app deployment:** SAP Mobile Services provides a cloud-based infrastructure for deploying and managing mobile apps.

© Pranay Gupta 2024
P. Gupta, *Digital Transformation of SAP Supply Chain Processes*,
https://doi.org/10.1007/979-8-8688-0270-6_4

- **Mobile app security:** SAP Mobile Services provides several features to help secure mobile apps, such as authentication, authorization, and data encryption.

- **Mobile app monitoring and analytics:** SAP Mobile Services provides several tools for monitoring and analyzing mobile app use.

# The Benefits of SAP BTP and SAP Mobile Services

- **Reduced development time:** SAP BTP and SAP Mobile Services provide several tools and services that can help developers build and deploy mobile apps more quickly and easily.

- **Improved performance and security:** AP BTP and SAP Mobile Services provide a cloud-based infrastructure that can help improve the performance and security of mobile apps.

- **Reduced costs:** SAP BTP and SAP Mobile Services can help businesses reduce the costs of developing and managing mobile apps.

- **Increased agility:** SAP BTP and SAP Mobile Services can help businesses be more agile and responsive to changing market conditions.

# The Variety of Apps Using SAP BTP and SAP Mobile Services

- **Customer-facing apps:** SAP Mobile Services can be used to develop customer-facing apps, such as product catalogs, e-commerce apps, and customer service apps.

- **Business Users apps:** SAP Mobile Services can be used to develop business user apps, such as supply chain, spend performance, and contract management apps.

- **Employee-facing apps:** SAP Mobile Services can be used to develop employee-facing apps, such as time and attendance apps, expense tracking apps, and Salesforce automation apps.

- **Field service apps:** SAP Mobile Services can be used to develop field service apps, such as mobile asset management apps, field service management apps, and customer service management apps.

- **Internet of Things (IoT) apps:** SAP Mobile Services can be used to develop IoT apps, such as remote monitoring and control apps, predictive maintenance apps, and data analytics apps.

# Tools and Services in SAP BTP

SAP BTP and SAP Mobile Services are a powerful combination of tools and services that can help businesses develop, deploy, and manage mobile apps more effectively. If you are looking for a way to accelerate your mobile development efforts and improve the performance and security of your mobile apps, you should consider using SAP BTP and SAP Mobile Services.

To configure SAP Mobile Services, you need to utilize XSUAA and SAP Cloud Connecter services.

# What Is XSUAA?

XSUAA, which stands for *Cross-Service User Account and Authentication*, is a component in the SAP Cloud Platform that provides user authentication and authorization services for applications and services running on the platform. It is commonly used to secure and manage user access to various SAP Cloud Platform services and applications.

Here are some key aspects of XSUAA:

- **User authentication:** XSUAA allows applications and services on the SAP Cloud Platform to authenticate users. It supports various authentication mechanisms, including basic authentication, OAuth 2.0, and SAML (Security Assertion Markup Language). This flexibility enables developers to integrate XSUAA with a wide range of identity providers and authentication methods.

- **Authorization and scopes:** XSUAA supports fine-grained authorization and access control. You can define authorization scopes and roles and assign them to users or user groups. This allows you to control which actions and resources a user can access within your application or service.

- **Single sign-on (SSO):** XSUAA supports single sign-on, which means that once a user is authenticated, they can access multiple services and applications on the SAP Cloud Platform without having to re-enter their credentials. This enhances user convenience and security.

- **Multi-tenancy support:** XSUAA can be configured to support multi-tenancy, allowing you to have multiple tenants or customer organizations using your applications, each with its own set of users and permissions.

- **Identity federation:** XSUAA can be configured to federate with external identity providers, allowing users to sign in using their existing credentials from another trusted source.

XSUAA is a critical component for developers and organizations building applications and services on the SAP Cloud Platform. It ensures that user access is properly authenticated and authorized, which is essential for securing sensitive data and resources in a cloud-based environment. It also simplifies user management and enables a consistent user experience across different applications and services within the platform.

# What Is SAP Cloud Connector?

The SAP Cloud Connector is a component of the SAP Cloud Platform that enables secure and reliable communication between on-premises systems and cloud applications running on the SAP Cloud Platform or other cloud-based services. It acts as a bridge between your on-premises systems and SAP's cloud-based services, allowing data to flow between them while maintaining security and connectivity.

Key features and functions of the SAP Cloud Connector include:

- **Secure connectivity:** The SAP Cloud Connector provides secure communication channels, often using encrypted connections, between your on-premises systems and the SAP Cloud Platform. This ensures that data transferred between these environments is protected.

- **Reverse invocation:** It allows cloud applications to initiate communication with on-premises systems, enabling real-time data access and integration between the two.

- **Firewall traversal:** The Cloud Connector can traverse firewalls and network boundaries, making it easier to integrate cloud applications with on-premises systems that might be located behind corporate firewalls.

- **Certificate management:** The Cloud Connector supports certificate management and authentication mechanisms to enhance security and trust between the on-premises systems and the cloud environment.

- **Scalability:** The Cloud Connector can be scaled and configured to support multiple on-premises systems and cloud applications, making it suitable for large and complex integration scenarios.

- **Configuration management:** Administrators can configure and manage the SAP Cloud Connector through a web-based interface, allowing them to define which on-premises systems and services are accessible from the cloud.

SAP Cloud Connector is a critical component for organizations that use SAP Cloud Platform and need to integrate their cloud applications with existing on-premises systems, such as ERP, databases, or other legacy applications. It helps ensure that data and processes can flow seamlessly between the two environments, facilitating hybrid cloud deployments and business process integration. See Figure 4-1.

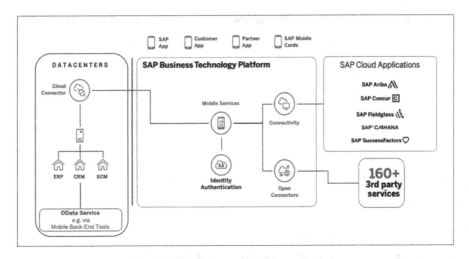

***Figure 4-1.***  *The SAP BTP and SAP Mobile Services architecture*

# Configuring SAP Mobile Services

For a perspective on configuration, I provide the detailed steps needed to configure the SAP Mobile Services in SAP BTP. Later examples use a different SAP Mobile Services account from a professional system.

1. Create a Trail account on `https://account.hana.ondemand.com`.

2. You need to create a global account and then a subaccount.

3. Enable the Cloud Foundry Environment.

4. Create a space and name, as per your requirements. See Figure 4-2.

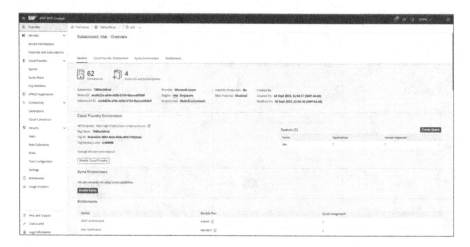

***Figure 4-2.*** *SAP BTP global account and subaccount*

5. Add Mobile Services to your subaccount and create an instance of Mobile Services. See Figure 4-3.

***Figure 4-3.*** *SAP Mobile Services in SAP BTP*

***Figure 4-4.*** *Creating a SAP Mobile Services instance in space*

***Figure 4-5.*** *SAP Mobile Services instance*

6.  Once the Mobile Service instance is up and running
    (see Figure 4-5), log in to Mobile Services cockpit
    and create a new hybrid app. This example creates
    a test app called SupplyChains. You need to provide
    a unique ID for your app. This example uses com.
    materialmobility. This ID would be used to
    establish connections from the frontend UI to the
    Mobile Services app configuration. See Figure 4-6.

*Figure 4-6.* *Hybrid Mobile application*

You need to add security settings for SSO and user
authentication, as shown in Figure 4-7.

***Figure 4-7.*** *Mobile App security settings*

***Figure 4-8.*** *Mobile App role settings*

This example uses the default XSUAA service and
the No Role setting to show the configuration (see
Figure 4-8). You can use security and authorization
settings as per your organization's security policies.
SAP Portal and SAP Basis consultants can help with
these settings.

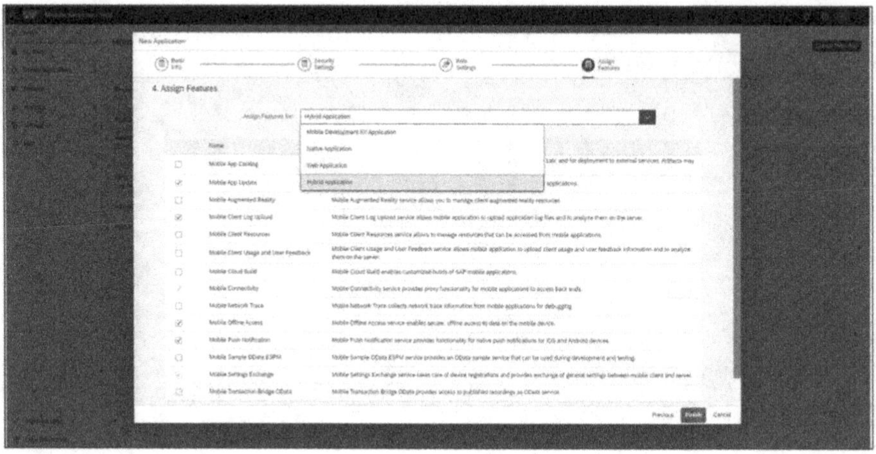

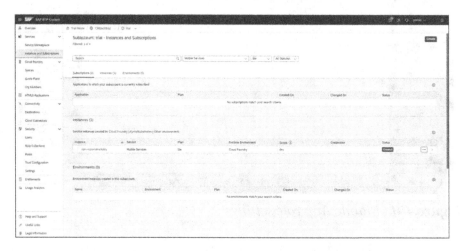

***Figure 4-9.*** *Mobile App features*

You can see the mobile services instance running in your trail subaccount, as shown in Figure 4-10.

***Figure 4-10.*** *Mobile App instance running in SAP BTP*

7. Now look at the newly created app. Because you
   used the OAuth security protocol, the system
   generated an authorization endpoint, a token
   endpoint, and an OAuth Client ID. These security
   and API links are used to connect to the app
   deployed on SAP Mobile Services. See Figures 4-11
   through 4-13.

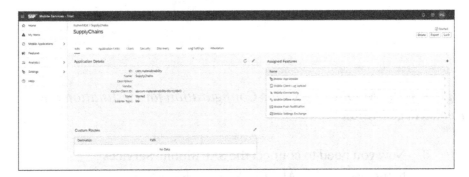

*Figure 4-11.* *Mobile App's basic information*

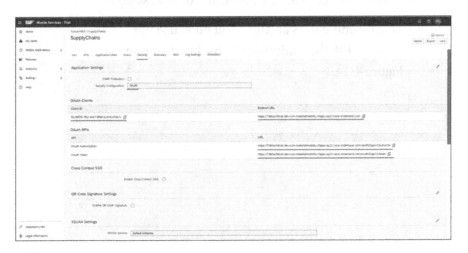

*Figure 4-12.* *Mobile App's OAuth client and API configuration*

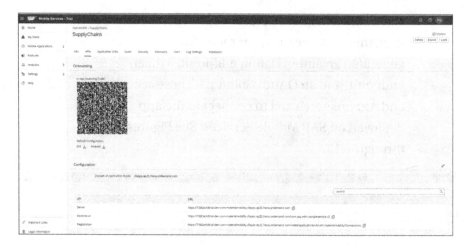

***Figure 4-13.*** *Mobile app's APIs Configuration for Destination and Device Registration*

8. Now you need to connect the SAP Mobile Services to the backend—SAP ECC. You need to create a destination in SAP BTP using a destination service. It will connect to the OnPremise SAP ECC system.

   This example uses an URL. You must use the correct URL that points to the backend system. See Figure 4-14.

***Figure 4-14.*** *RFC destination to the backend SAP ECC system*

---

**Note**   These examples use OnPremise SAP ECC as the backend system where the OData services reside. SAP Mobile Services can connect to other ERP systems or databases as well.

This requires SAP Cloud Connector to be set up in the client's system landscape. Cloud Connector configurations are not covered in this book.

---

9.   Add this new destination in the Mobility app to point to the OData URLs. Once it's authenticated correctly using the Cloud Connector and XSUAA configurations, this URL will connect to the actual OData services and will allow data exchange between the backend and the frontend. See Figures 4-15 and 4-16.

**Figure 4-15.**  *Mobile application connectivity configuration*

**Figure 4-16.**  *OData URL in the backend SAP ECC system*

10.    You can configure Mobile Exchange Policies as per
the company security policies. See Figure 4-17.

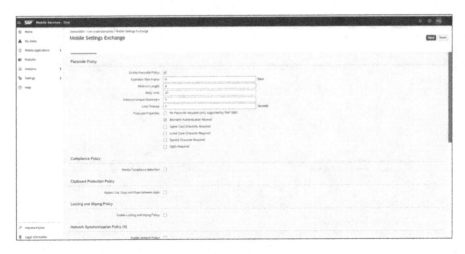

*Figure 4-17.* *Mobile settings exchange configuration*

# Test Service for Purchase Order Details and Goods Receipt Using the POSTMAN API Client

This example uses the Professional Mobile Services system. It is connected with an identity provider and integrated with the backend SAP ECC system where the OData services are hosted.

Say you created a purchase order with two serialized line items in the SAP ECC system, as shown in Figure 4-18.

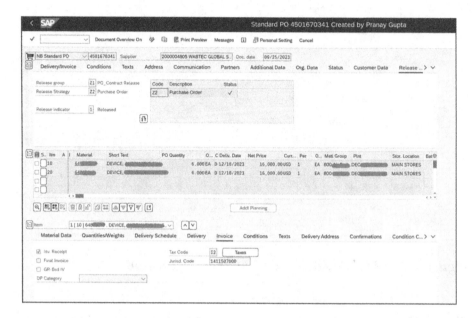

***Figure 4-18.***  *Purchase order in SAP*

Now you can use the POSTMAN tool to test the OData services.

First, you need to get a CSRF token using a metadata service or other service with the GET method. (You'll learn about CSRF and the CORS protocol in Chapter 5.) You need to add the OAuth authorization endpoints that were generated in Mobile Services so that you can authenticate and pass through the SAP Mobile Services system. This example uses the OAuth 2.0 protocol for connection. See Figures 4-19 and 4-20.

```
https://mobile-XXXXXXXXXX.us2.hana.ondemand.com/GW_dest/sap/
opu/OData/SAP/ZMIM_GR_APP_SRV/$metadata
```

**Figure 4-19.**  *OAuth setup in POSTMAN*

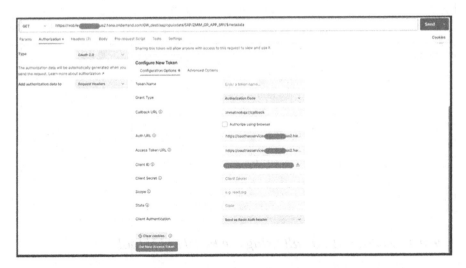

**Figure 4-20.**  *OAuth setup in POSTMAN - token configuration*

Now get a new access token, as shown in Figure 4-21.

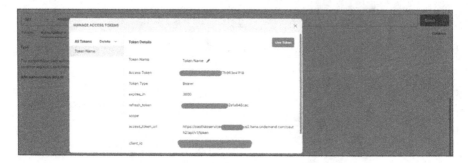

*Figure 4-21.* *OAuth token details*

*Figure 4-22.* *Metadata call using the POSTMAN tool*

Now get the details of the purchase order using the PO details service.

```
https://mobile-XXXXXXXXXX.us2.hana.ondemand.com/GW_dest/
sap/opu/OData/SAP/ZMIM_GR_APP_SRV/GRHeaderSet(MatDoc='',
DocYear='',PoNumber='4501670341')?X-SMP-APPID=com.xx.xx.
materialmobility&sap-client=100&$expand=GRHeadertoItem/
GRItemToGRItemComp,GRHeadertoItem/GRItemToGRItemSrno
```

***Figure 4-23.*** *Purchase order details using the POSTMAN tool*

Figure 4-23 shows the response from the OData service with the purchase order details.Now you post the Goods Receipt using the POST method, like you did in the previous steps when testing the services as standalone from the SAP Gateway system. Use the response received from the PO details service as requested in the XML body. You have to pass the X-CSRF-TOKEN that you received from the previous metadata call or GET call for the PO details.

You can `fetch` the CSRF token, as shown in the GET method in Figure 4-24.

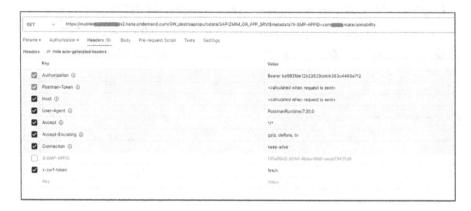

***Figure 4-24.*** *CSRF token request in the POSTMAN tool*

This example posts all six quantities on both items with the serial numbers listed in Table 4-1.

***Table 4-1.*** *Transfer Posting Serial Numbers List*

| Item 1 Serial Numbers | Item 2 Serial Numbers |
| --- | --- |
| IMEISERIAL121 | IMEISERIAL127 |
| IMEISERIAL122 | IMEISERIAL128 |
| IMEISERIAL123 | IMEISERIAL129 |
| IMEISERIAL124 | IMEISERIAL130 |
| IMEISERIAL125 | IMEISERIAL131 |
| IMEISERIAL126 | IMEISERIAL132 |

```
https://mobile-XXXXXXXXXX.us2.hana.ondemand.com/GW_dest/sap/
opu/OData/SAP/ZMIM_GR_APP_SRV/GRHeaderSet
```

You have to pass the CSRF token received in the previous metadata call in the header. Otherwise, you'll get a CSRF token validation failed error. See Figure 4-25.

***Figure 4-25.*** *CSRF token response in the POSTMAN tool*

***Figure 4-26.*** *Create Goods Receipt using the POSTMAN tool*

***Figure 4-27.*** *Goods Receipt document response using the POSTMAN tool*

Figure 4-27 shows that the Goods Receipt document 5003868986 has been posted successfully, with all the serial numbers provided in the OData response. See Figures 4-28 and 4-29.

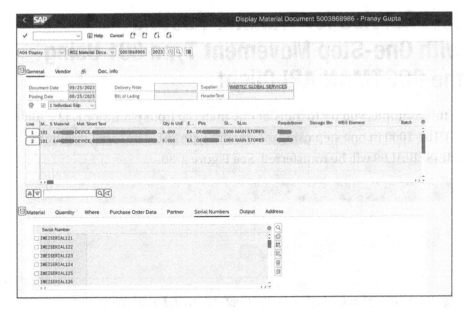

*Figure 4-28.*  *Goods Receipt document—first item details*

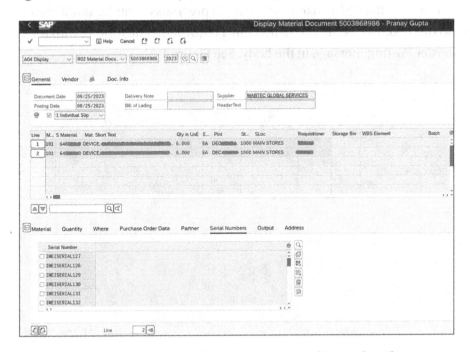

*Figure 4-29.*  *Goods Receipt document—second item details*

# Test Service for Transfer Posting with One-Step Movement Type 301 Using the POSTMAN API Client

In this example, you try to transfer one material from plant sloc C423-1000 to C102-1000 in one step using movement type 301. The serial number IMEISERIAL69 will be transferred. See Figure 4-30.

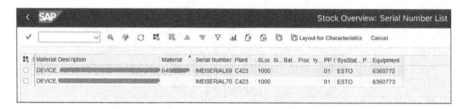

*Figure 4-30.*   *Stock in plant C423 before transfer posting*

You'll get the CSRF token as you did in previous example, You'll then pass this token as a query parameter in a request message along with the Transfer Posting message in the body. See Figure 4-31.

***Figure 4-31.*** *CSRF token request*

```
https://mobile-XXXXXXXXXX.us2.hana.ondemand.com/GW_dest/sap/
opu/OData/SAP/ZMIM_GR_APP_SRV/GTHeaderSet
```

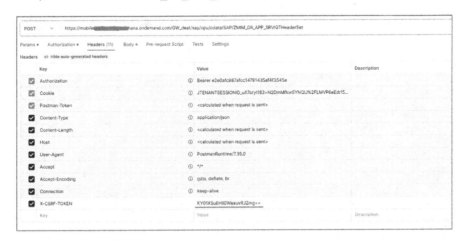

***Figure 4-32.*** *CSRF token response*

**Figure 4-33.** *Request JSON message for Transfer Posting—movement type 301*

**Figure 4-34.** *Transfer Posting document—movement type 301*

The Transfer Posting document 4908644267 has been posted successfully. See Figure 4-35.

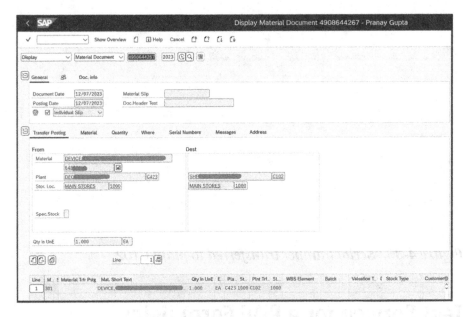

***Figure 4-35.***  *Transfer Posting document overview*

The serial number has been transferred to plant C102-1000, as shown in Figure 4-36.

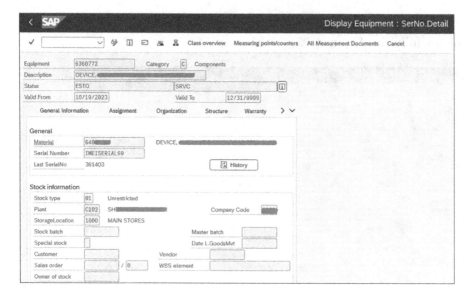

*Figure 4-36.*  *Serial number transferred to plant C102*

# Test Service for a PDF Form Using the POSTMAN API Client

https://mobile-XXXXXXXXXX.us2.hana.ondemand.com/GW_dest/sap/
opu/OData/SAP/ZMIM_GR_APP_SRV/PDFLabelcopy(Mblnr='5003868986',
Mjahr='2023',Mblpo='')?&filter(Printer eq 'Z')

***Figure 4-37.*** *PDF label service test using the POSTMAN tool*

**Figure 4-38.** *Goods Receipt PDF label*

# CHAPTER 5

# Working with the Ionic and Angular Frameworks to Build iOS Apps

Ionic and Angular are two popular web development frameworks often used in combination to create modern and feature-rich web and mobile applications. This chapter explores each of these frameworks in more detail.

## The Angular Framework

Angular is a comprehensive and widely adopted frontend JavaScript framework developed and maintained by Google. It provides a structured and organized way to build dynamic, single-page web applications (SPAs) and web-based enterprise applications. Here are some key features and components of Angular:

- **Modular architecture:** Angular applications are built using modules that encapsulate different parts of the application's functionality, making it easier to manage and scale.

© Pranay Gupta 2024
P. Gupta, *Digital Transformation of SAP Supply Chain Processes*,
https://doi.org/10.1007/979-8-8688-0270-6_5

- **Components:** Angular introduces the concept of components, which are self-contained, reusable building blocks for user interfaces. Each component typically includes HTML templates, TypeScript code, and CSS styles.

- **Dependency injection:** Angular includes a powerful dependency injection system that helps manage the creation and sharing of application components and services.

- **Two-way data binding:** Angular offers two-way data binding, which means that changes to the application's data automatically update the user interface, and user interactions can also update the data.

- **Directives:** Angular provides directives like ngIf, ngFor, and ngSwitch, which allow you to manipulate the DOM and add dynamic behavior to templates.

- **Services:** Services are used for sharing data and logic between different parts of an Angular application. They are often used for tasks like making HTTP requests and managing state.

- **Routing:** Angular's router allows for building single-page applications with multiple views. It provides features like route parameters, lazy loading, and guards for controlling access to routes.

- **Form handling:** Angular offers powerful form-handling capabilities with features like form validation, template-driven forms, and reactive forms.

- **Testing:** Angular has a robust testing ecosystem, with tools like Jasmine and Protractor for writing unit tests and end-to-end tests.

- **TypeScript:** Angular is built using TypeScript, a statically typed superset of JavaScript. TypeScript offers strong type checking and helps catch errors at compile-time, enhancing code quality and maintainability.

- **RxJS integration:** Angular incorporates RxJS (Reactive Extensions for JavaScript) for handling asynchronous operations and data streams. This allows for more efficient and responsive applications, particularly when dealing with real-time data.

- **Internationalization (i18n):** Angular provides built-in support for internationalization and localization. Developers can easily translate their applications into multiple languages to reach a global audience.

- **Angular CLI:** The Angular command-line interface (CLI) simplifies project setup, code generation, testing, and deployment tasks. It streamlines the development workflow, making it easier for developers to get started.

- **Angular Universal:** Angular Universal is a technology that allows for server-side rendering (SSR) of Angular applications. SSR improves performance, search engine optimization (SEO), and initial page load times.

- **Enterprise adoption:** Angular is often chosen for enterprise-scale applications due to its comprehensive features, strong tooling, and long-term support from Google.

# The Ionic Framework

Ionic is an open-source framework for building cross-platform, mobile applications using web technologies such as HTML, CSS, and JavaScript/TypeScript. It is often described as a "hybrid" framework because it allows developers to build native-like mobile apps that can run on multiple platforms, including iOS, Android, and the web. Here are some key features of Ionic:

- **UI components:** Ionic provides a rich set of pre-designed UI components that look and feel like native mobile elements. These components are styled using CSS and can be easily customized.

- **Cross-platform development:** Developers can use a single codebase to build mobile apps for multiple platforms, reducing development time and effort.

- **Native access:** Ionic provides a set of plugins and APIs that allow access to native device features like the camera, GPS, and device sensors. These plugins bridge the gap between web technologies and native functionality.

- **Angular integration:** Ionic is often used in conjunction with Angular, and it provides Angular integration out of the box. Developers can use Angular to build the business logic of their mobile apps while leveraging Ionic for the user interface.

- **Themability:** Ionic apps are highly *themable*, and developers can create custom themes or use existing ones to match the branding and design requirements of their apps.

- **Performance:** Ionic apps are known for good performance, thanks to optimizations like ahead-of-time (AOT) compilation and lazy loading.

- **Community and ecosystem:** Ionic has a large and active community, which means access to a wealth of tutorials, plugins, and resources. There's also an Ionic marketplace for additional components and services.

- **Platform agnostic:** Ionic apps can run on multiple platforms, including iOS, Android, and the web, using a single codebase. This reduces development costs and allows for consistent user experiences across devices.

- **PWA support:** Ionic provides Progressive Web App (PWA) support, enabling applications to work offline, be installed on home screens, and offer responsive design for various screen sizes.

- **Live reload:** Developers can use Ionics' live reload feature to see changes in real-time during development, making the development and testing processes more efficient.

- **Ionic capacitor:** While Ionic originally relied on Cordova, it has since introduced Capacitor, a modern native runtime that allows for building cross-platform apps with even better performance and extensibility.

- **Appflow:** Ionic offers a cloud-based DevOps platform called Ionic Appflow. It provides features like automated builds, app deployment, continuous integration (CI), and monitoring for Ionic apps.

- **Enterprise-ready:** Ionic offers enterprise-level support, security features, and integration options, making it suitable for businesses building mission-critical applications.

In summary, Angular is a robust frontend framework for building web applications, while Ionic is a framework for building cross-platform mobile apps using web technologies. When used together, Angular and Ionic provide a powerful combination for creating web and mobile applications that share code and resources, making development more efficient and cost-effective.

# Cordova Plugins

A Cordova plugin, also known as a PhoneGap plugin (since Cordova was formerly known as PhoneGap), is a piece of native code that provides an interface between a Cordova-based mobile app and the native device features and functionality of a mobile platform, such as iOS or Android. Cordova plugins allow developers to access and utilize native device capabilities that are not available through web technologies alone, such as accessing the camera, GPS, accelerometer, and more.

Here are some key characteristics and aspects of Cordova plugins:

- **Access to native features:** Cordova plugins act as bridges between JavaScript code in your mobile app and native code written in languages like Objective-C (iOS) or Java (Android). They enable your app to utilize device-specific capabilities and interact with hardware and software components.

- **Modularity:** Cordova plugins are designed to be modular. You can add and remove them as needed, reducing the app's overall size and complexity.

- **Plugin architecture:** Each Cordova plugin consists of JavaScript code that defines a consistent API and native code implementations for various platforms. The JavaScript API is accessible from your app's JavaScript code, making it easy to call native functionality.

- **Installation:** To use a Cordova plugin, you typically install it using the Cordova CLI or a package manager like npm. This process includes adding the plugin to your project and configuring it as needed.

- **Plugin APIs:** Cordova plugins expose specific APIs that you can use in your app. For example, a camera plugin might provide methods for taking photos, while a geolocation plugin might offer functions for accessing the device's GPS data.

- **Platform compatibility:** Cordova plugins are platform-specific, meaning that you might need to find or develop separate plugins for iOS and Android if the native APIs differ significantly between the two platforms.

- **Plugin updates:** The availability and functionality of Cordova plugins can change over time, as the underlying mobile platforms evolve. Developers need to ensure that they use up-to-date and well-maintained plugins.

- **Custom plugin development:** If you require functionality not covered by existing Cordova plugins, you can create custom plugins by writing native code for the target platforms and exposing JavaScript APIs.

In summary, Cordova plugins are essential components in the development of hybrid mobile applications. They enable developers to extend the capabilities of their apps beyond what web technologies alone can offer, allowing for seamless integration with native device features and functionalities.

You can find more information on the following pages:

```
https://angular.io/
https://ionic.io/
https://cordova.apache.org/
```

# SupplyChains App Functions

This section focuses on the functions that have been added to the Mobile app. This includes supply chain functions like Goods Receipts, Goods Issues, Transfer Posting reports, Stock on Hand reports (MB52), Document Cancelation reports, and Reprint labels. There are different ways to create Goods Receipts—using a standard purchase order versus a subcontract purchase order, using outbound delivery to complete the GR for a Stock Transport order, or using a transfer document generated for movement type 303.

Let's first look at the Goods Receipt screen using a standard PO.

# The Goods Receipt Function

This section uses a new PO (number 4501670430) in SAP ECC and uses it for the Goods Receipt function.

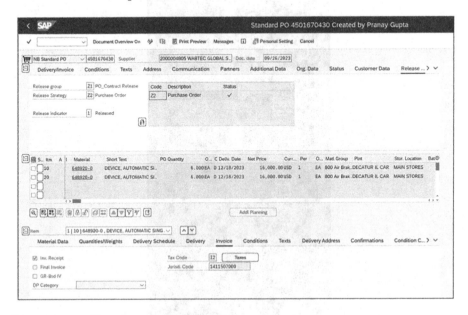

***Figure 5-1.*** *Purchase order in SAP*

Log in to the app and open the Goods Receipt option. Then select the Standard/SubContract PO option and enter the PO number. Click Create.

***Figure 5-2.*** *Mobile app functions*

***Figure 5-3.*** *The Create Goods Receipt screen*

**Figure 5-4.** *PO Number input field*

***Figure 5-5.*** *Barcode scanning*

This is where app will establish the connection with the SAP Mobile Services, as explained in the "Registering and Deleting Devices on the SAP Mobile Server" topic later in this chapter.

Frontend applications are responsible for passing the IMEI numbers of devices, along with other user account identity data, such as phone numbers and emails, which organizations like to store in the SAP Mobile Services system logs for any security investigations or when analyzing other application issues.

If the PO number is available in the form of a barcode from the vendor, you can use this number with the Scan function to populate the PO number in the field.

***Figure 5-6.*** *PO Number confirmation*

***Figure 5-7.*** *PO details screen*

Once the connection is established, the app will call the PO details service using the PO number and the PO details will be passed and presented on the screen. Before the PO details, you need to call the metadata service to get the CSRF tokens so that data can be exchanged safely between frontend and backend systems. The importance and use of a CSRF token is explained in the "CSRF Token" topic later in this chapter. Also, an example of CSRF token exchange is shown while testing the services in "Test Service for Purchase Order Details and Goods Receipt Using the POSTMAN API Client" topic in Chapter 4.

Users can select the item and view the details to make sure that they are receiving the correct items.

Users have the flexibility to modify the desired quantity for reception. When receiving serialized items, users must input the corresponding serial numbers. Additionally, if suppliers provide serial numbers in a barcoded format, users can conveniently scan and input them for efficient processing.

Implement frontend validations wherever feasible to minimize the necessity of invoking the OData service continuously, thereby mitigating potential performance concerns. For instance, consider a frontend validation that ensures the uniqueness of serial numbers on the screen. When the same serial number is detected, an error should be prompted, compelling users to input distinct serial numbers. Although SAP's backend BAPIs also enforce this control, repeatedly sending data with incorrect serial numbers to the backend and receiving errors post-submission will result in a suboptimal user experience.

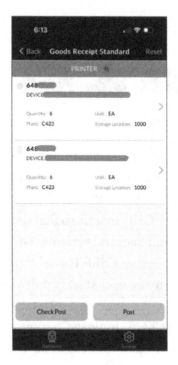

*Figure 5-8.* *PO items list*

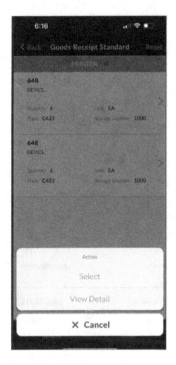

***Figure 5-9.*** *PO item list selection*

***Figure 5-10.***  *PO items overview*

***Figure 5-11.*** *PO items actions*

***Figure 5-12.*** *Serial number input*

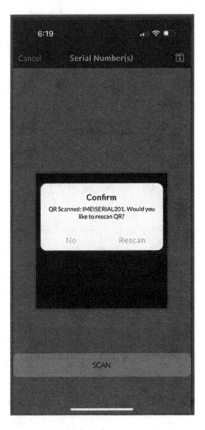

*Figure 5-13.*  *Serial number scan*

**Figure 5-14.**  *PO items list*

***Figure 5-15.***  *Document check confirmation*

The Check Post button simulates the Check function provided in the **MIGO** transaction in SAP. This function is available in the Goods Movement BAPI, which ensures that all data errors are removed before passing the data to the backend systems.

Once the Document Check is successful, the Post Button is enabled and you can post the document.

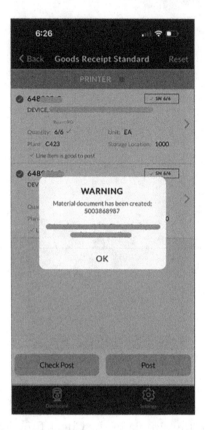

***Figure 5-16.*** *Goods Receipt document*

If you check the document in SAP in **MIGO**, you should see that it successfully posted the Goods Receipt against PO 4501670430.

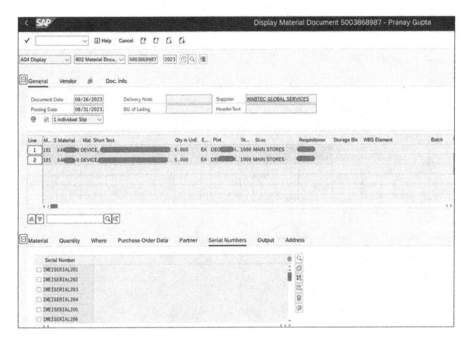

*Figure 5-17.* *Goods Receipt document overview – line item 1*

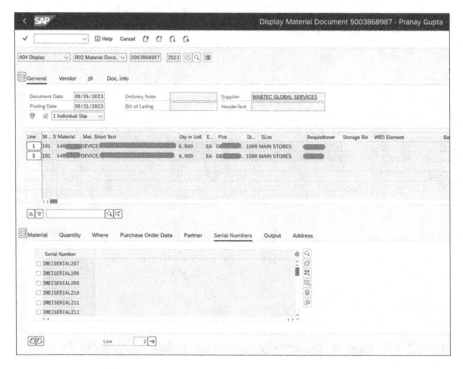

***Figure 5-18.*** *Goods Receipt document overview – line item 2*

# The Transfer Posting Function

The options for movement types 301, 303, 311, and 313 for Transfer Posting are available under the Transfer Posting tile. These represent one-step (301 and 311) for one-step movement types and the first step (303 and 313) for two-step movement types.

Second-step movements (305 and 315) have been integrated into Goods Receipt (Place in Storage) in the Goods Receipt tile with selection Transfer.

User-friendly screens have been designed with all the fields required to perform Transfer Postings from one plant sloc to another plant sloc.

# Movement Type 301 (One-Step Transfer)

The following screen shots cover movement type 301 using the Mobile app.

This example performs a Transfer Posting of two quantities using the one-step transfer movement type 301.

| From Plant | From Sloc | To Plant | To Sloc |
|---|---|---|---|
| C423 | 1000 | C102 | 1000 |

This example follows the transfer-posting rules as governed by SAP t-code **MIGO**. It uses the same serialized material for transfer.

*Figure 5-19.*  *Transfer Posting options*

***Figure 5-20.*** *Header details*

*Figure 5-21.*  *Item details*

***Figure 5-22.*** *Quantity input*

Because this is serialized material, it includes frontend validation for serial numbers to be provided.

This service also includes another service that imports all the serial numbers available in the From store. For example, if you are transferring the serial numbers from C423-1000, this service will populate all the serial numbers in inventory in C423-1000. This will help users choose the correct serial numbers rather than randomly typing in the serial numbers and getting an error at the time of posting.

***Figure 5-23.*** *Adding serial numbers*

*Figure 5-24.* *Serial number details*

***Figure 5-25.***  *Select the serial numbers*

***Figure 5-26.***  *Serial number check*

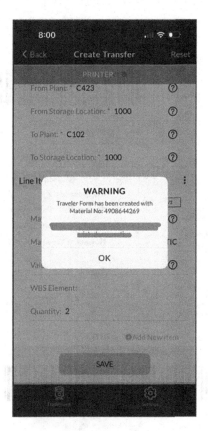

***Figure 5-27.*** *Transfer Posting document*

Transfer Posting document 4908644269 has been posted successfully. The Traveler form has also been designed in 4*3 format, which means it can be printed as a label on a Zebra printer.

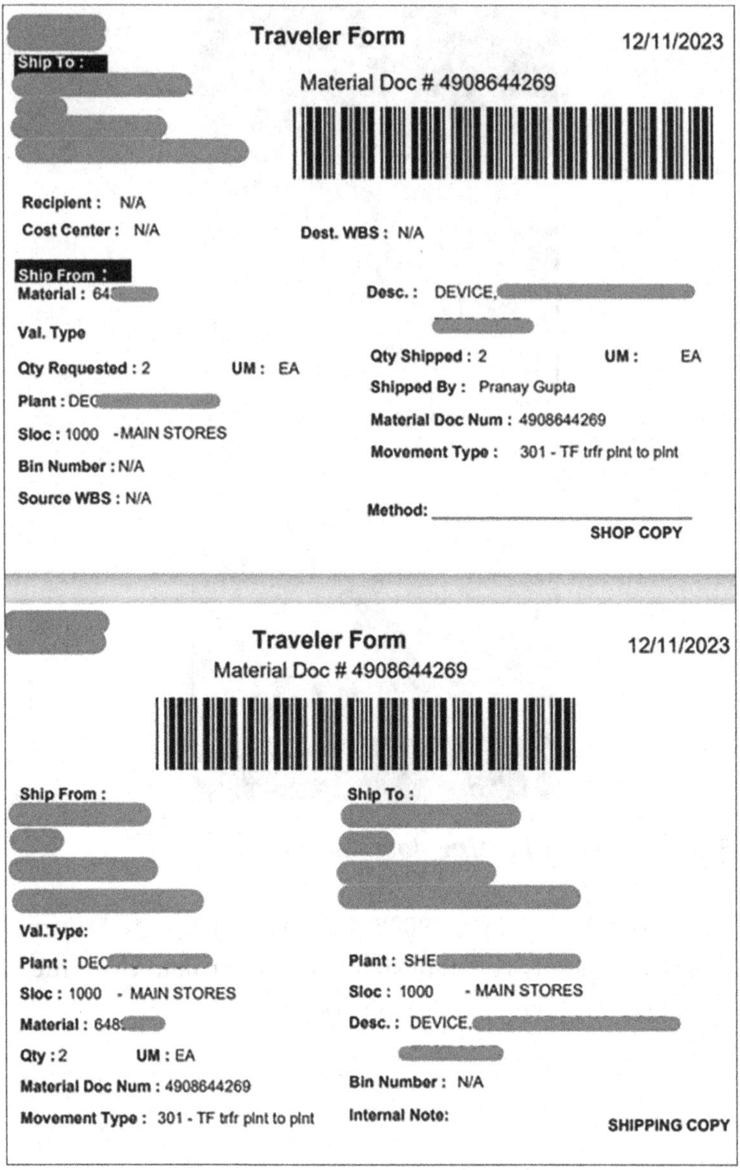

[redacted]

**Traveler Form** 12/11/2023

**Ship To :**

[redacted]

Material Doc # 4908644269

**Recipient :** N/A

**Cost Center :** N/A

**Dest. WBS :** N/A

**Ship From :**

**Material :** 64[redacted]

**Desc. :** DEVICE,[redacted]

**Val. Type**

**Qty Requested :** 2 **UM :** EA

**Qty Shipped :** 2 **UM :** EA

**Plant :** DE[redacted]

**Shipped By :** Pranay Gupta

**Sloc :** 1000 -MAIN STORES

**Material Doc Num :** 4908644269

**Bin Number :** N/A

**Movement Type :** 301 - TF trfr plnt to plnt

**Source WBS :** N/A

**Method:** ______________________

**SHOP COPY**

[redacted]

**Traveler Form** 12/11/2023

Material Doc # 4908644269

**Ship From :**

[redacted]

**Ship To :**

[redacted]

**Val.Type:**

**Plant :** DE[redacted]

**Plant :** SHE[redacted]

**Sloc :** 1000 - MAIN STORES

**Sloc :** 1000 - MAIN STORES

**Material :** 648[redacted]

**Desc. :** DEVICE,[redacted]

**Qty :** 2 **UM :** EA

**Material Doc Num :** 4908644269

**Bin Number :** N/A

**Movement Type :** 301 - TF trfr plnt to plnt

**Internal Note:**

**SHIPPING COPY**

***Figure 5-28.*** *Traveler form - movement type 303*

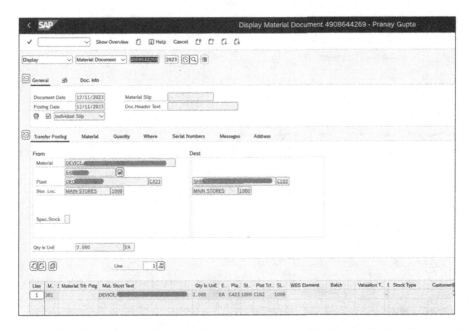

***Figure 5-29.***   *Transfer Posting document overview - movement type 301*

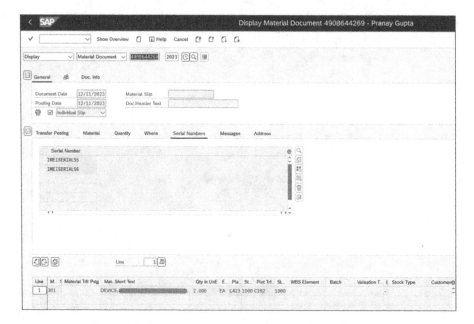

***Figure 5-30.*** *Transfer Posting document - serial number details*

Both serial numbers have been transferred to C102-1000 successfully.

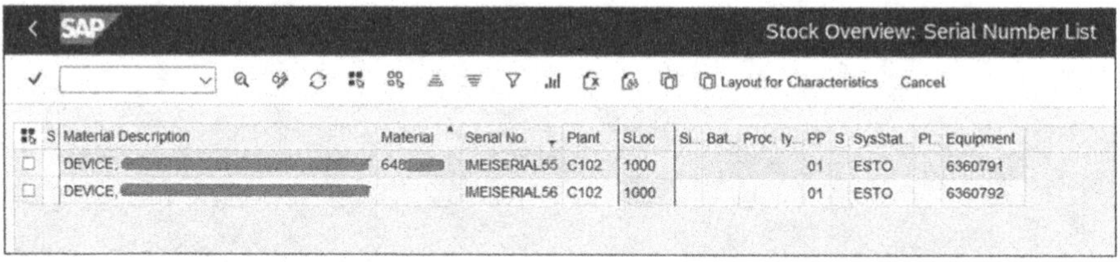

***Figure 5-31.*** *Stock in plant C102 after Transfer Posting*

All other movement types, such as 303, 311, and 313, follow the same design with the corresponding fields available in **MIGO**.

This example also introduces the Valuation Type field, a critical feature alongside serialization for materials. You can use valuation types like NEW, REFURB, and many others, as configured in SAP Customizing.

# Movement Types 313 and 315 (Two-Step Transfer)

This example performs a Transfer Posting of two quantities using the two-step transfer movement types 313 and 315.

| From Plant | From Sloc | To Plant | To Sloc |
|------------|-----------|----------|---------|
| C423 | 1000 | C423 | 1001 |

The first step is posted using movement type 313 from the app, as you saw for movement type 301.

***Figure 5-32.*** *Header and item details*

***Figure 5-33.*** *Document - movement type 313*

Transfer Posting document 4908644273 has been posted successfully for movement type 313 as the first step. The Traveler form has also been designed in 4*3 format, which means it can be printed as a label on a Zebra printer.

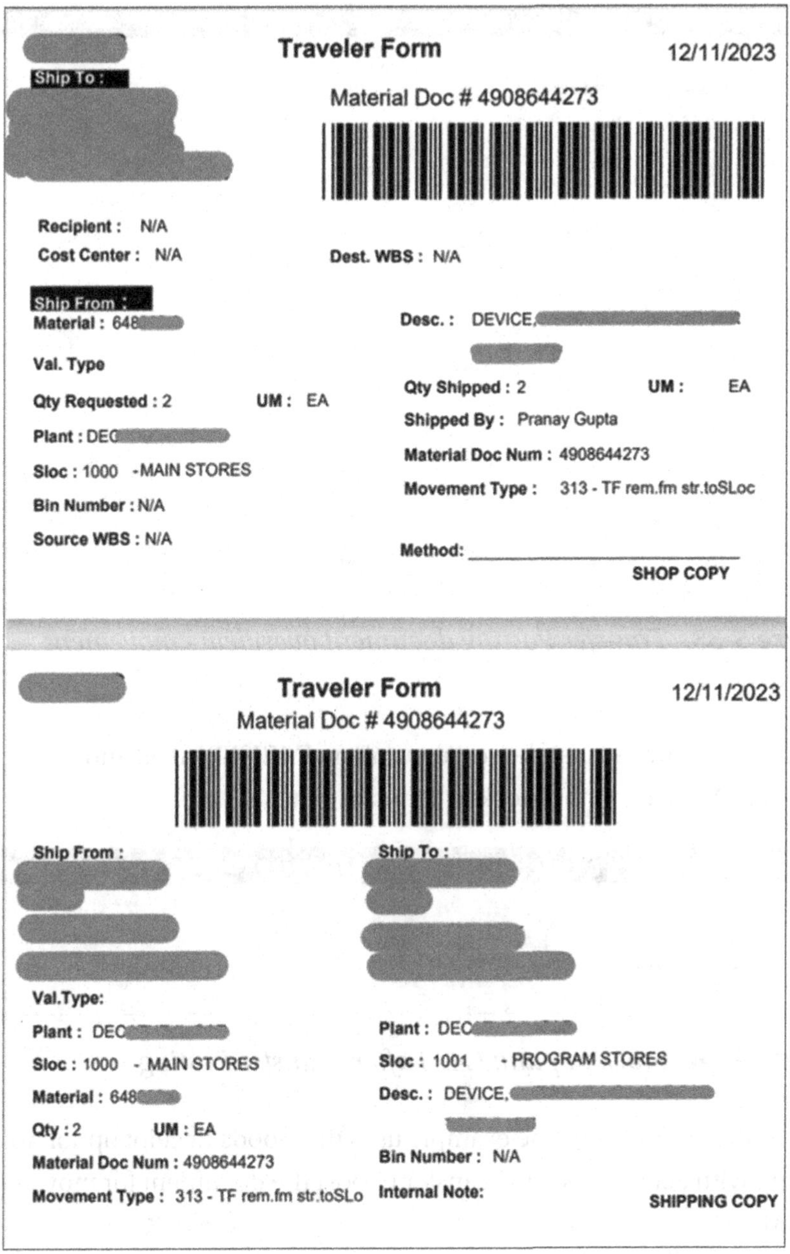

*Figure 5-34.* *Traveler form - movement type 313*

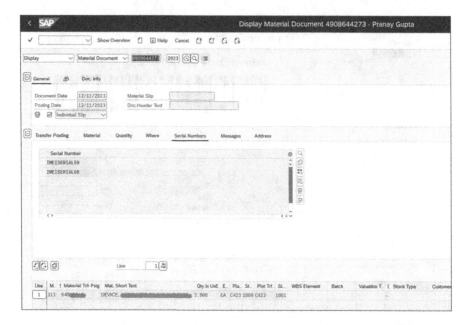

***Figure 5-35.*** *Transfer Posting document overview - movement type 313*

You can now see that the serial numbers IMEISERIAL59 and IMEISERIAL60 are in the Stock In Transfer state.

| S | Material Description | Material | Serial Number | Plant | SLoc | Sl.. | Bat.. | Proc. ty.. | PF | S | SysStat.. | Pl.. | Equipment |
|---|----------------------|----------|---------------|-------|------|------|-------|------------|----|---|-----------|------|-----------|
| ☐ | DEVICE, | 648 | IMEISERIAL59 | C423 | 1001 | | | | 04 | | ESTO | | 6360795 |
| ☐ | DEVICE, | 648 | IMEISERIAL60 | C423 | 1001 | | | | | | ESTO | | 6360796 |

***Figure 5-36.*** *Stock in plant C423 after Transfer Posting*

For the second step, the example uses the Goods Receipt option in the app with Selection set to Transfer to post the document for movement type 315.

*Figure 5-37.* *Material document input*

***Figure 5-38.*** *Item list from movement type 313*

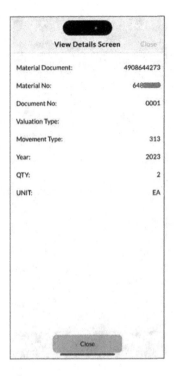

***Figure 5-39.*** *Item details*

*Figure 5-40.* *Document - movement type 315*

Transfer Posting document 4908644274 has been posted successfully for movement type 315 as the second step. The Traveler form has also been designed in 4*3 format, which means it can be printed as a label on a Zebra printer.

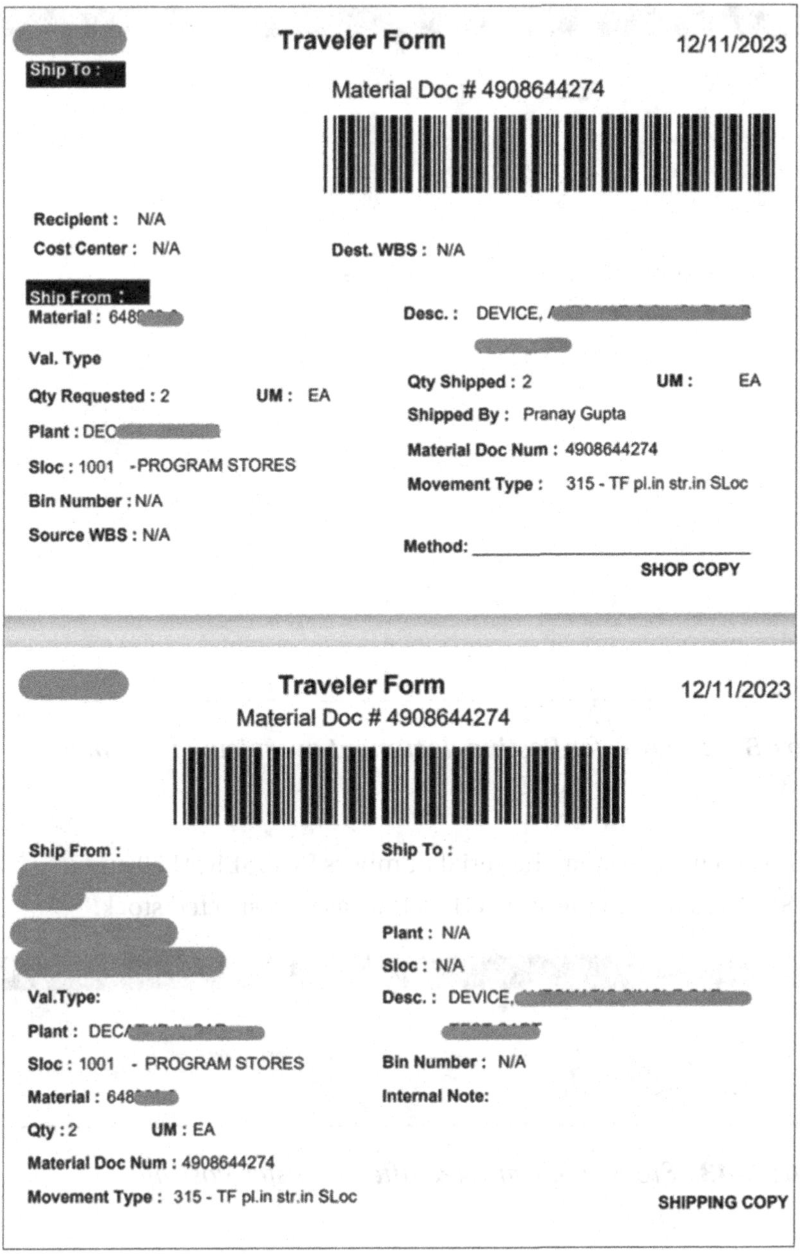

**Traveler Form** 12/11/2023

Ship To :

Material Doc # 4908644274

Recipient :  N/A
Cost Center :  N/A

Dest. WBS :  N/A

Ship From :
Material : 648

Desc. :  DEVICE, A

Val. Type

Qty Requested : 2  UM :  EA

Qty Shipped : 2  UM :  EA

Shipped By :  Pranay Gupta

Plant : DEC

Material Doc Num : 4908644274

Sloc : 1001  -PROGRAM STORES

Movement Type :  315 - TF pl.in str.in SLoc

Bin Number : N/A

Source WBS : N/A

Method: _____

SHOP COPY

**Traveler Form** 12/11/2023

Material Doc # 4908644274

Ship From :

Ship To :

Plant :  N/A

Sloc :  N/A

Val.Type:

Desc. :  DEVICE,

Plant : DECA

Sloc : 1001  - PROGRAM STORES

Bin Number :  N/A

Material : 648

Internal Note:

Qty : 2  UM : EA

Material Doc Num : 4908644274

Movement Type :  315 - TF pl.in str.in SLoc

SHIPPING COPY

*Figure 5-41.* *Traveler form - movement type 315*

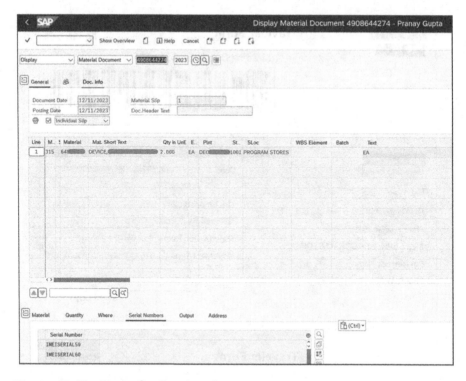

***Figure 5-42.*** *Transfer Posting document overview - movement type 315*

You can now see that the serial numbers IMEISERIAL59 and IMEISERIAL60 are in the store C423-1001 as unrestricted stock.

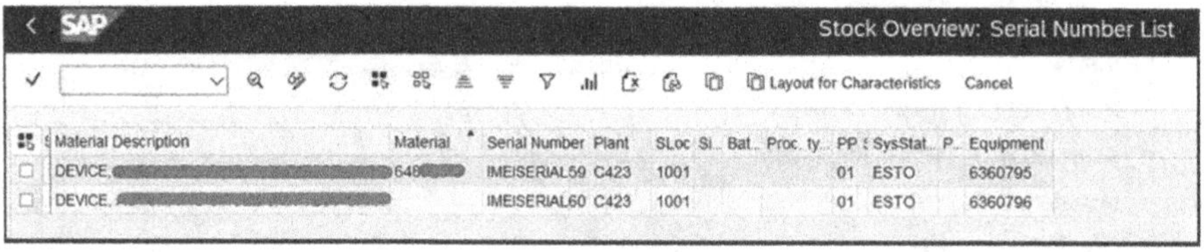

***Figure 5-43.*** *Stock in plant C423 after Transfer Posting*

# The Goods Issue Function

This section shows you how to use the Goods Issue function to issue serial numbers IMEISERIAL57 and IMEISERIAL58 to cost center 60302.

| | Material Description | Material | Serial Number | Plant | SLoc | Si. | Bat. | Proc. ty. | PP | SysStat. | P. | Equipment |
|---|---|---|---|---|---|---|---|---|---|---|---|---|
| ☐ | DEVICE. | 64 | IMEISERIAL70 | C423 | 1000 | | | | 01 | ESTO | | 6360773 |
| ☐ | DEVICE. | | IMEISERIAL57 | C423 | 1000 | | | | 01 | ESTO | | 6360793 |
| ☐ | DEVICE. | | IMEISERIAL58 | C423 | 1000 | | | | 01 | ESTO | | 6360794 |

*Stock Overview: Serial Number List*

***Figure 5-44.*** *Stock in plant C423 before Transfer Posting*

Use the Goods Issue function on the app with movement type 201.

***Figure 5-45.*** *Mobile app functions*

*Figure 5-46.*  *Cost center GI - movement type 201*

*Figure 5-47.*  *Cost center item details*

*Figure 5-48.* *Serial number details*

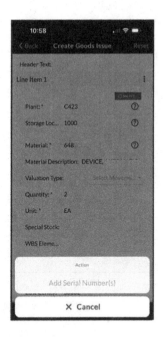

**Figure 5-49.** *Adding serial numbers*

***Figure 5-50.*** *Serial number selection*

Once all the relevant fields for Goods Issues are provided—such as Cost Center, Plant, Sloc, Material, and Quantities—you can post the document.

***Figure 5-51.*** *Goods Issue document*

You can see the two quantities issued to the cost center with movement type 201 using t-code **MB51**.

***Figure 5-52.*** *Material document report - MB51*

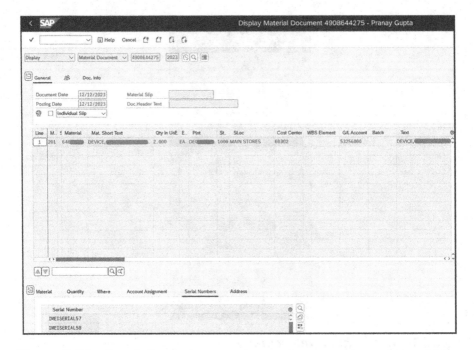

***Figure 5-53.*** *Goods Issue document overview - movement type 201*

On the same screen of Goods Issue, you can post movement type 221, which is Goods Issue to WBS. You also need to provide the WBS element number to post the document.

# Additional Functions

In addition to these essential supply chain functions, this service incorporates user-friendly features that ensure a seamless experience, delivering maximum value to the users.

These functions have been added as different entities in the same OData service; however, you could instead create separate OData services for each of these functions.

This example leverages various validation services to ensure accurate data retrieval from the backend system, preventing users from utilizing incorrect information. For example, search help services exist for valid plants, storage locations, valuation types, material numbers, descriptions, vendors, open POs, document types, user ID searches, storage bins, and many other fields. These services are important to ensure the data integrity of the goods movement documents.

# The PO Search Function

This search is based on SAP t-code **ME2N**.

Usage:

- **Display purchase orders**: ME2N is primarily used to display and view information related to purchase orders. Users can enter specific criteria such as the PO number, document date, vendor, or other parameters to retrieve relevant PO data.

- **Filtering options:** The transaction provides various filtering options, allowing users to narrow down the list of displayed purchase orders. Filters can be applied based on parameters like document type, vendor, document date, and more.

- **Document overview:** ME2N offers a document overview that includes key details such as the PO number, vendor information, document date, status, and other relevant data. Users can navigate through the list and select a specific PO for detailed analysis.

- **Document history:** Users can view the history of changes made to a purchase order, providing a detailed audit trail of modifications.

- **Output control: ME2N** allows users to control and configure the output of information, such as printing purchase orders or exporting data to different formats for reporting purposes.

- **Goods receipt and invoice receipt:** The transaction provides information on Goods Receipts and invoice receipts related to a purchase order.

Key fields and parameters:

- **Document date:** Specifies the date of the purchase order document.

- **Vendor:** Users can enter the vendor code to filter purchase orders related to a specific vendor.

- **Material:** Filters purchase orders based on the material number.

- **Plant and sloc:** Filters purchase orders based on plant and storage location.

Benefits:

- **Purchase order visibility: ME2N** provides a quick and efficient way to view and analyze purchase orders, enhancing visibility into procurement activities.

- **Audit trail:** The ability to view the history of changes made to a purchase order supports auditing and compliance requirements.

- **Decision support:** Helps in making informed decisions related to procurement and order management.

You can also restrict the search to show open POs that are pending for Goods Receipt. This will help users focus on POs that are pending in their store, and they can follow up with vendors about fulfilment.

***Figure 5-54.*** *Search functions*

***Figure 5-55.*** *PO search screen*

# The Inventory Search Function

This search is based on SAP t-code **MB52**.

Usage:

- **Stock analysis: MB52** is primarily used for analyzing material stocks in the SAP system. It provides detailed information about the current stock levels, stock values, and various other key metrics.

- **Material and plant selection:** Users can specify a particular material and plant for which they want to review the stock details. This allows for a more focused analysis of stock data.

- **Stock types:** The transaction provides a breakdown of stocks based on different stock types, such as unrestricted stock, blocked stock, and in-transit stock. This helps users understand the status of materials in the warehouse.

- **Valuation views: MB52** offers different valuation views, allowing users to assess stock values based on different accounting principles or methods, such as standard price, moving average price, or other valuation methods configured in SAP.

- **Historical data:** Users can also retrieve historical stock data by specifying a particular date or a range of dates. This feature is useful for tracking changes in stock levels over time.

- **Exporting data: MB52** allows users to export stock data to external formats such as Excel for further analysis or reporting purposes.

Key fields and parameters:

- **Material:** Enter the material code for which you want to view stock details.

- **Plant:** Specify the plant code to narrow down the analysis to a specific plant.

- **Stock type:** Filter stocks based on different stock types.

- **Valuation level:** Choose the valuation level for stock valuation.

- **Date:** Specify a specific date or date range for historical stock data.

Benefits:

- **Inventory visibility:** Provides a comprehensive view of material stocks, aiding in inventory visibility.

- **Decision support:** Helps in making informed decisions related to inventory management and procurement.

- **Audit and compliance:** Supports auditing processes by providing a detailed stock history and valuation information.

This example provides a basic search for stock, which can help store supervisors look at their stock in real time.

***Figure 5-56.*** *Inventory search list*

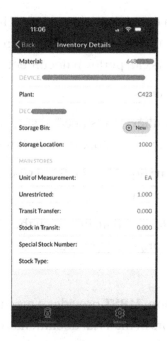

*Figure 5-57.*  *Result list item details*

# The Doc Reversal Function

This function is based on SAP t-code **MBST**.

Usage:

- **Material document cancellation: MBST** is primarily used to cancel material documents in the SAP system. Material documents are records of goods movements, such as Goods Receipts, Goods Issues, or stock transfers.

- **Document reversal:** The transaction allows users to reverse previously posted material documents. This reversal can be necessary in case of errors, incorrect postings, or if there is a need to undo a goods movement.

197

- **Authorization control:** Access to **MBST** is controlled through SAP authorization roles to ensure that only authorized users can perform document cancellations.

Key fields and parameters:

- **Document number:** Users need to enter the document number of the material document they want to cancel.

- **Document year:** Specifies the fiscal year of the material document to be canceled.

- **Document date:** The date on which the material document was originally posted.

Benefits:

- **Error correction: MBST** provides a mechanism for correcting errors in material documents, ensuring accurate recording of goods movements.

- **Reversal of goods movements:** Allows for the reversal of Goods Receipts, Goods Issues, and other material document postings.

- **Audit trail:** The cancellation reason and the reversal of material documents create an audit trail for tracking changes in the system.

Let's try to cancel the document 4908644268, which is movement type 301.

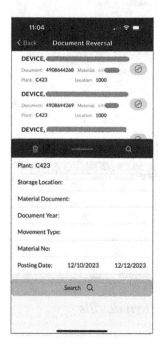

**Figure 5-58.** *Document reversal list*

***Figure 5-59.*** *Result list item details*

***Figure 5-60.*** *Reversal document*

Cancelation document 4908644279 has been posted with movement type 302, which is a reversal document for movement type 301.

This will move the serial numbers IMEISERIAL51 and IMEISERIAL51 back from C102 1000 to C423 1000.

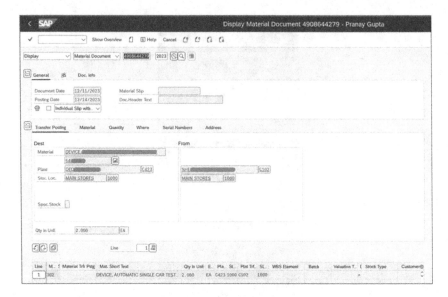

***Figure 5-61.*** *Reversal document details - movement type 302*

# Angular Code Snippets for Establishing Connections to SAP Mobile Services

This part of the chapter shows examples of Angular and Ionic code for special functions that are required to connect this app to SAP Mobile services and to make it useful for business users.

# Registering and Deleting Devices on the SAP Mobile Server

Registering a device on the SAP Mobile Server is an essential step in mobile application development when you're using SAP's Mobile platform to build and deploy mobile apps that interact with SAP systems or other backend services. Registering a device allows the Mobile Server to recognize and manage the mobile device's interactions securely.

When you create a new app in Mobile Server, the system generates the API to connect to mobile services from the mobile end client. Follow these steps:

1. Log in. First you need to log in to SAP Mobile Services using an authorization endpoint URL. Most of the mobile development kits and frameworks have standard methods for authentication using the OAuth security protocol.

   For this example app, the following OAuth APIs were generated.

   ```
   https://7380acfdtrial-dev-com-
   materialmobility.cfapps.ap21.hana.ondemand.
   com/oauth2/api/v1/authorize
   ```

   ```
   https://7380acfdtrial-dev-com-
   materialmobility.cfapps.ap21.hana.ondemand.
   com/oauth2/api/v1/token
   ```

   After you log in successfully to SAP Mobile Services through configured IDP (Identity Provider)/AD account services, you need to register the device.

2. Register the device. For this example app, the following API was generated to register the device on an exchange server. You can use this API with the CREATE method to create new registrations.

   ```
   https://7380acfdtrial-dev-com-
   materialmobility.cfapps.ap21.hana.
   ondemand.com/OData/applications/v4/com.
   materialmobility/Connections
   ```

The registration service will return the registration
ID, which will be used as a header parameter
X-SMP-APPCID while calling individual OData
services from the app. Device registration needs
to be checked every time before exchanging data.
You need to make sure that you don't add duplicate
registrations of the same device.

3.  Delete the registration. Before logging out, you need
    to delete the device registration. You can use this
    API with the DELETE method to delete the existing
    registration ID for your device.

    ```
    https://7380acfdtrial-dev-com-
    materialmobility.cfapps.ap21.hana.
    ondemand.com/OData/applications/
    v4/com.materialmobility/
    Connections(REGISTRATION_ID)
    ```

4.  Log out. At the close of the app, you need to
    close all sessions on the SAP Mobile Server so
    that all the tokens are reset and new connections
    are established at the time of next launch. This
    is important step. Otherwise, there will be
    unnecessary sessions of Mobile Server running,
    which may cause issues with data exchange and
    degrade Mobile Server performance.

    ```
    https://7380acfdtrial-dev-com-
    materialmobility.cfapps.ap21.hana.ondemand.
    com/mobileservices/sessions
    ```

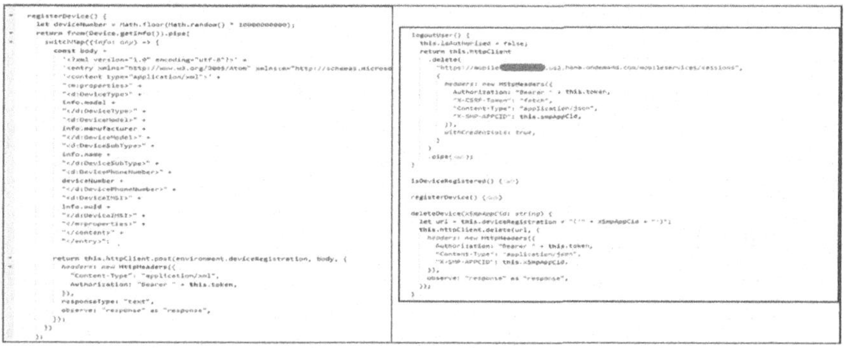

**Figure 5-62.**  *Angular code snippets for registration and deletion of devices in the SAP Mobile Server*

Examples of individual OData URLs for data exchange are shown in Figure 5-63.

```
export class Environment {
  environment = ⬤;
  production = false;
  mockdata = false;
  envPath = "GW_dest";
  setMockdata = (bool) => {
    this.mockdata = bool;
  };

  /** feature flags */
  hideReceiptList = false;
  hideTransferPosting = false;
  hideTransferReversal = false;
  hideGoodsIssue = false;
  hideGoodsIssueReversal = false;
  request_timeout = 60000;

  basicAuthorizationDetails = "";
  xsmpappcid = "";

  // SAP Mobile Services Configuration
  clientId = "███████████0128";
  redirectUri = "immatmobqa://callback";
  applicationId = "com██████.materialmobility";

  ██████URL
  baseURL = "https://mobile-██████us2.hana.ondemand.com";
  discoveryUrl = "████████████████████";
  deviceRegistration = `${this.baseURL}/odata/applications/v4/${this.applicationId}/Connections`;
  logoutUrl = `${this.baseURL}/mobileservices/sessions`;
  searchPO = `${this.baseURL}/${this.envPath}/sap/opu/odata/SAP/ZMIM_GR_APP_SRV/POSearchSet?`;
  inventoryLookup = `${this.baseURL}/${this.envPath}/sap/opu/odata/sap/ZMIM_GR_APP_SRV/InventSearchSet?`;
  searchGI = `${this.baseURL}/${this.envPath}/sap/opu/odata/SAP/ZMIM_GR_APP_SRV/GIListSet?sap-client=100&`;
  stockInTransit = `${this.baseURL}/${this.envPath}/sap/opu/odata/SAP/ZMIM_GR_APP_SRV/StockInTransitSet?`;

  travelerFormPrint = `${this.baseURL}/${this.envPath}/sap/opu/odata/sap/ZMIM_GR_APP_SRV/GTZebraTFSet`;
  reversal = `${this.baseURL}/${this.envPath}/sap/opu/odata/SAP/ZMIM_GR_APP_SRV/CancelDocSet`;
  receiptList = `${this.baseURL}/${this.envPath}/sap/opu/odata/sap/ZMIM_GR_APP_SRV/GRListSet?sap-client=100&`;
  transferList = `${this.baseURL}/${this.envPath}/sap/opu/odata/SAP/ZMIM_GR_APP_SRV/GTTransferListSet?$format=json&`;
  binList = `${this.baseURL}/${this.envPath}/sap/opu/odata/sap/ZMIM_GR_APP_SRV/BinLabelSet?`;
  binSave = `${this.baseURL}/${this.envPath}/sap/opu/odata/sap/ZMIM_GR_APP_SRV/BinTransferSet`;
  binPrint = `${this.baseURL}/${this.envPath}/sap/opu/odata/sap/ZMIM_GR_APP_SRV/BinLabelSet`;
```

*Figure 5-63. Angular code snippets for individual OData URLs for data exchange*

Registered devices can be monitored in the Mobile Settings Exchange, under Mobile App configurations. Registered devices and users can be blocked or deleted from the SAP Mobile Server as well.

*Figure 5-64.*  *SAP Mobile Server logs*

# Barcode Scanning

You can add a Barcode function to the app to scan PO numbers and
serial numbers. This example uses Cordova/Capacitor plugins to add this
feature.

```
import { Injectable } from "@angular/core";
import {
  BarcodeScanner,
  ScanResult,
} from "@capacitor-community/barcode-scanner";


async startScan() {
  try {
    const canScann = await this.checkPermission();
    if (canScann) {
      this.scanActive = true;
      BarcodeScanner.hideBackground();
      const result = await BarcodeScanner.startScan();
      if (result.hasContent) {
        debugger;
        console.log("Scan result:", result);
        this.confirmScannedQR(result);
      } else {
        console.error("No data from scanner", result);
      }
    } else {
      console.warn("Not allowed to scan");
    }
  } catch (e) {
    console.error("Error with scanner", e);
  } finally {
    this.scanActive = false;
  }
}
```

```
confirmScannedQR(result: ScanResult) {
  this.utilService
    .displayAlert(
      SupplyChainMessage.TITLE_CONFIRM,
      `QR Scanned: ${result.content}. Would you like to rescan QR?`,
      [AlertButtonText.NO, AlertButtonText.RESCAN]
    )
    .subscribe((buttonIndex) => {
      if (buttonIndex === 2) {
        this.startScan();
        return;
      }
      this.scanResult.next(result.content);
      this.scanActive = false;
    });
}


async checkPermission() {
  return new Promise(async (resolve, reject) => {
    const status = await BarcodeScanner.checkPermission({ force: true });
    if (status.granted) {
      resolve(true);
    } else if (status.denied) {
      const alert = await this.alertController.create({
        header: "No Permission",
        message: "Please allow camera access in your settings",
        buttons: [
          { text: "No", role: "cancel" },
          {
            text: "Settings",
            handler: () => {
              resolve(false);
              BarcodeScanner.openAppSettings();
            },
          },
        ],
      });
    });
}
```

*Figure 5-65.*  *Angular code snippets for barcode scanning*

# Using CSRF Tokens

A *CSRF* (Cross-Site Request Forgery) token, also known as an anti-CSRF token or synchronizer token, is a security feature used in web applications to protect against Cross-Site Request Forgery attacks. CSRF attacks occur when a malicious website or script tricks a user's web browser into making an unintended and potentially harmful request to another website where the user is authenticated. To prevent CSRF attacks, web applications use CSRF tokens. These tokens are random, unique values generated for each user session or each individual request. The server embeds this token into forms or includes it as a request header. When the user submits a form or makes a request, the server verifies that the CSRF token sent with the request matches the expected one. If they don't match or if the token is missing, the server rejects the request as potentially malicious.

Before the first OData call, you need to get a CSRF token from the server. You can use this token until it expires. This token needs to be passed as header parameter X-CSRF-TOKEN. These token settings are set in SAP Mobile Server, as shown in Chapter 4.

Figure 5-66 shows an example for a GET call that fetches the X-CSRF-TOKEN from Mobile Server. The POST call then uses the same token to post the data.

```
return this.httpClient.get(url, {          checkPost(payload: any, token: string, opType: string) {
  headers: new HttpHeaders({                 if (this.env          ) {
    "Content-Type": "application/xml",          return this.httpClient.get(                   );
    "X-CSRF-Token": "Fetch",                 } else {
  }),                                          const url =
  responseType: "text",                          opType === "transfer"
  observe: "response" as "response",             ? this.env.postGTHeader
  withCredentials: true,                         : this.env.postGRHeaderSet;
});                                          return this.httpClient.post(url, payload, {
                                               headers: new HttpHeaders({
                                                 "Content-Type": "application/json",
                                                 "X-CSRF-Token": token,
                                               }),
                                               withCredentials: true,
                                             });
```

***Figure 5-66.*** *Angular code snippets for CSRF token retrieval*

# CORS Protocol/Capacitor Configuration

CORS stands for "Cross-Origin Resource Sharing." It is a security feature implemented by web browsers that controls how web pages in one domain can request and interact with resources (such as data and services) hosted on another domain. CORS is a crucial mechanism for web security and helps prevent certain types of attacks, such as Cross-Site Request Forgery (CSRF) and Cross-Site Scripting (XSS) attacks.

You might encounter CORS errors while exchanging data between iOS devices and SAP Mobile Services. To avoid CORS protocol errors, you need to add iosScheme and hostname to the capacitor config. You can also add the SAP Mobile Services hostname to the hostname field. See Figure 5-67.

```
1 ▾ {
2       "appId": "com      .eammaterial",
3       "appName":      material",
4       "bundledWebRuntime": false,
5       "npmClient": "npm",
6       "webDir": "www",
7 ▾     "plugins": {
8 ▾       "SplashScreen": {
9             "launchShowDuration": 5000,
10            "launchAutoHide": true,
11            "showSpinner": false,
12            "iosSpinnerStyle": "small",
13            "spinnerColor": "#999999"
14        }
15      },
16 ▾    "server": {
17        "iosScheme": "https",
18        "hostname": "mobile             .us2.hana.ondemand.com"
19      },
20      "cordova": {}
21 }
```

*Figure 5-67.*  *Angular code snippets for capacitor configuration*

# Label Printing with the Zebra Native Print App

This method prints labels that are created in SAP in Adobe and converted to Base64 format, then sent through OData services to the frontend app. That way, they can be printed on a Zebra printer.

210

This approach has an advantage of using existing labels and print output forms that were created in SAP and transmitting them using Xstring (XML) or Base64 format.

You can find details about Zebra Printer connectivity with iOS at the following link.

```
https://www.zebra.com/us/en/support-downloads/printer-
software/printer-setup-utilities.html
```

The printer is linked to the iPhone through Bluetooth connectivity. In the previous demonstration, you saw a system-generated notification indicating that the printer was not in a connected state. In the application's codebase, this example implements a feature that signifies the printer's status using a red icon when it is not connected, and a green icon when it is connected.

Furthermore, this application introduces a REPRINT functionality. This feature serves as a valuable resource in situations where the printer encounters difficulties in printing a document during the initial attempt after the document's submission. The inclusion of the REPRINT function is of significance due to the possibility of encountering unforeseen connectivity issues, which could result in the printer being non-operational during the initial document submission. In these cases, users have an alternative means to reprint their documents.

This example configures a Zebra printer to print the Goods Receipt Label in the 4*3 format. Once the printer is connected, you can choose the 4*3 dimension in the media settings for the Label/Tag option.

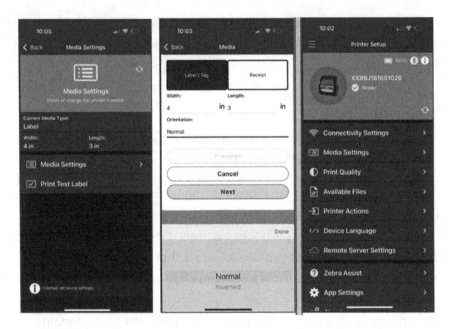

*Figure 5-68.*  *iOS Zebra Print app*

It is also important that the Goods Receipt label (the Adobe form) is created in similar dimensions in SAP.

You need to detect the Zebra printer status in the app and send the PDF GR Label output for printing. A prerequisite to this is that Zebra printer should be connected to the iPhone using Bluetooth. You can use available Zebra libraries to work with printer functions. This example created a custom plugin for this app.

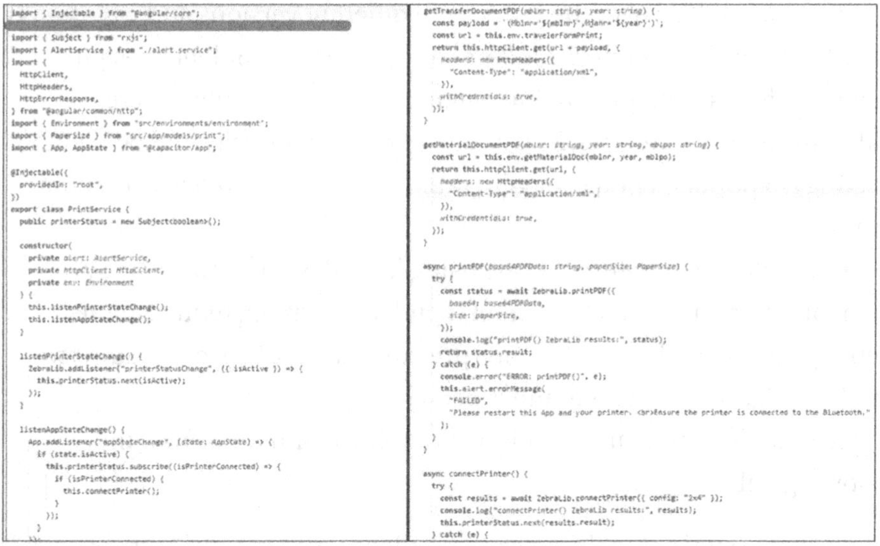

**Figure 5-69.** *Angular code snippets for Zebra printer detection and printing labels*

# Label Printing Using ZPL

ZPL, or the Zebra Programming Language, is a programming language specifically designed for creating labels and barcodes to be printed on Zebra label printers. These printers are commonly used for tasks such as printing shipping labels, product labels, and barcodes in various industries, including manufacturing, logistics, and retail.

ZPL is a command-based language that allows you to define the layout and content of labels to be printed. You can use a combination of text, graphics, and barcodes in ZPL to create customized labels to suit your specific needs. ZPL commands are typically embedded within a text document, and when sent to a compatible Zebra printer, they instruct the printer on how to generate the desired label.

ZPL has evolved over the years, with different versions and variations for different printer models. It offers various features for label design, including font selection, rotation, alignment, and the ability to create different types of barcodes. ZPL is known for its simplicity and efficiency, making it a popular choice for generating labels and barcodes on Zebra printers.

Users often generate ZPL code using label design software or by manually creating the code to meet their label printing requirements. Zebra printers are designed to interpret and execute ZPL commands to produce high-quality labels and barcodes.

You can find more information about ZPL commands from the following link:

```
https://support.zebra.com/cpws/docs/zpl/zpl-zbi2-pm-en.pdf
```

Using this approach, you can create labels in ZPL and then send these labels directly to the printer from the app.

To scan and connect the Bluetooth printer without having to create your own plugin, you can use the Bluetooth-le plugin provided by the Capacitor community.

You can use different methods of this plugin to scan, connect, and print to Bluetooth Zebra printers. See Figure 5-70.

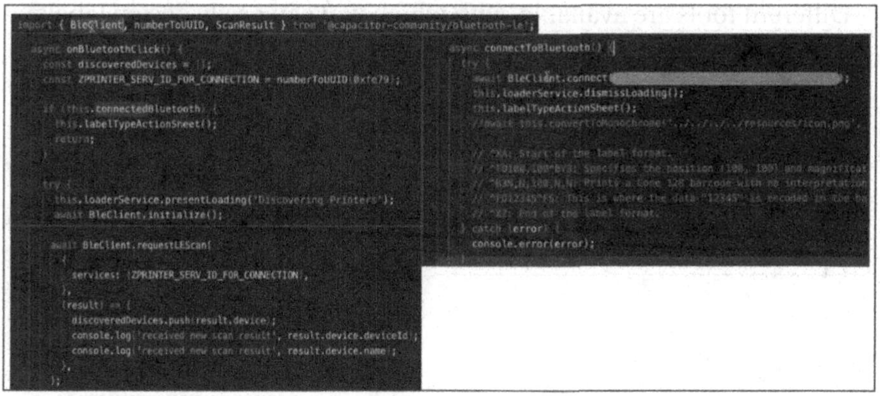

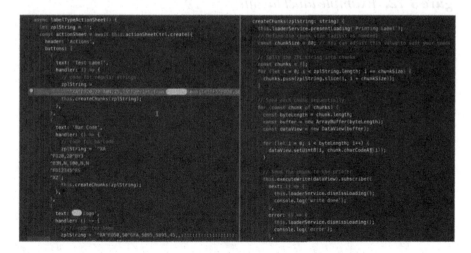

**Figure 5-70.** *Angular code snippets for Zebra label printing using ZPL*

You can create a label in ZPL and store it in a string, which can be passed to the printer for printing. Zebra printers can print labels created in ZPL. You can pass constant values and variables for individual labels in ZPL.

**Figure 5-71.** *Angular code snippets for Zebra label printing using ZPL*

215

Different tools are available, with which you can easily design labels and test them in ZPL—for example, check out `Labelary.com`.

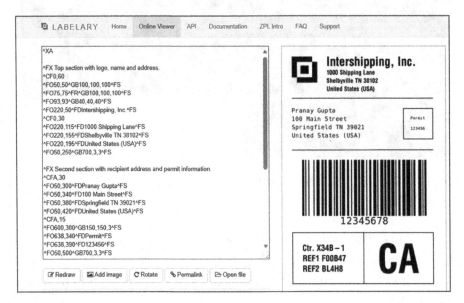

***Figure 5-72.** Example label layout*

# CHAPTER 6

# Attachments

Attachments play a crucial role in SAP, particularly in the context of purchase orders and Goods Receipts. They offer several benefits that enhance documentation, transparency, and communication throughout the procurement process. Here are some of the key reasons why attachments are important in SAP for purchase orders and Goods Receipts:

- Attachments allow organizations to maintain comprehensive records related to purchase orders and Goods Receipts. This documentation is essential for auditing, compliance, and historical reference.

- Attachments can include supporting documents such as invoices, packing slips, quality certificates, and other relevant files. These documents provide additional context and evidence for the transactions, helping in dispute resolution and verification.

- In many industries and regions, there are legal and regulatory requirements regarding the documentation and retention of transaction-related data. Attachments assist in meeting these compliance requirements by storing all relevant documents.

© Pranay Gupta 2024
P. Gupta, *Digital Transformation of SAP Supply Chain Processes*,
https://doi.org/10.1007/979-8-8688-0270-6_6

- Attachments can be used for data validation and verification. For example, invoices can be attached to Goods Receipts to ensure that the goods were received as per the purchase order and the corresponding invoice.

# What Is SAP DMS?

The SAP Document Management System (DMS) is a comprehensive solution offered by SAP that is designed to manage and control documents and content within the context of SAP business processes. It enables organizations to efficiently handle documents, attachments, and information related to their operations, ensuring data consistency, compliance, and streamlined business processes.

Here are the key features and functionalities of the SAP Document Management System:

- **Document storage:** DMS allows organizations to store various types of documents and content, including text documents, spreadsheets, images, CAD drawings, and more. These documents can be linked to specific SAP objects, such as customers, vendors, materials, purchase orders, and invoices.

- **Integration with SAP business documents:** DMS is tightly integrated with SAP business documents, like Purchase Orders, Invoices, Goods Receipts, Work Orders, and other legal documents, thereby ensuring that documents are directly associated with relevant SAP transactions and master data. This integration maintains data consistency and provides a complete view of information within the SAP ecosystem.

- **Document versioning:** DMS supports document versioning, enabling users to keep track of document revisions. This is essential for maintaining audit trails, tracking changes, and ensuring document accuracy.

- **Access control:** Robust access control mechanisms allow organizations to define permissions and security settings for documents. Access can be restricted based on user roles and responsibilities, ensuring data security and compliance with privacy regulations.

- **Workflow integration:** Documents stored in DMS can be seamlessly integrated into SAP workflows. This means that documents can be automatically routed, reviewed, and approved as part of business processes, improving efficiency and reducing manual handling.

- **Search and retrieval:** DMS provides powerful search and retrieval capabilities, allowing users to quickly find documents based on various criteria, including document type, date, keywords, and associated SAP objects.

- **Archiving and retention:** DMS includes an archiving functionality to manage the long-term storage and retention of documents, helping organizations comply with legal and regulatory requirements.

- **Document collaboration:** DMS facilitates document collaboration by allowing multiple users to work on documents simultaneously, with features like check-in and check-out to prevent conflicts.

- **Scalability:** The system is scalable to accommodate growing document storage needs, ensuring that organizations can handle increasing volumes of digital content efficiently.

- **Document lifecycle management:** DMS supports the entire document lifecycle, from creation and revision to archiving and disposal, ensuring that documents are managed throughout their lifespan.

- **Compliance and audit:** DMS helps organizations meet compliance and audit requirements by providing a structured and auditable way to store, manage, and access documents.

- **Performance optimization:** By storing documents separately from the SAP database, DMS can optimize the performance of the core SAP system, especially when dealing with large volumes of documents.

In summary, SAP Document Management System (DMS) is a powerful tool that enhances document management, data integrity, workflow automation, and compliance within the SAP environment. It empowers organizations to efficiently handle their documents and content while seamlessly integrating them into their business processes.

# Configuring SAP DMS

This example uses SAP DMS with IBM Content Manager, which is an external content repository. In this scenario, you'll add images to one of the mobile apps, which is configured to send attachments to external content repositories on partition YB using SAP DMS configurations. These attachments will be added in functional locations or maintenance notifications.

1. **Configure an external repository using t-code OAC0.** You need to add the content server address here. The content server should be reachable with the HTTP protocol from the SAP system. This can be configured by Basis Consultants.

*Figure 6-1.* *External Repository Name*

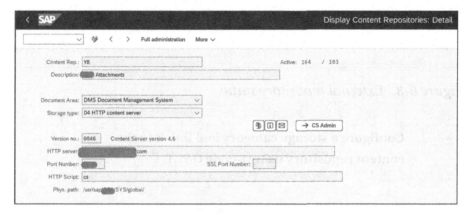

*Figure 6-2.* *External repository HTTP configuration*

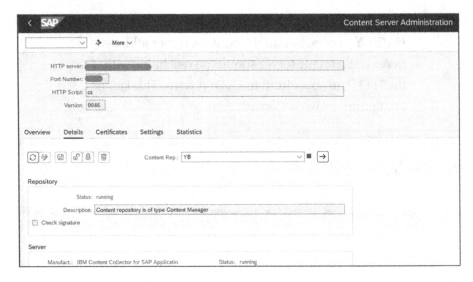

***Figure 6-3.*** *External repository status*

2.   **Configure a storage category and link it to the content repository using t-code OACT.**

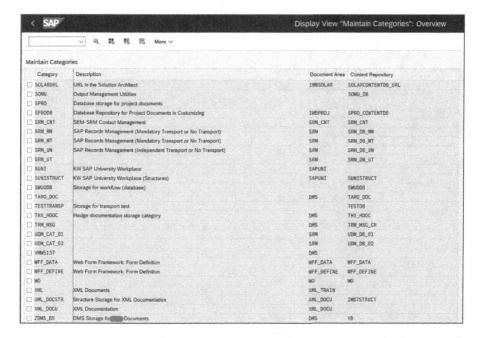

*Figure 6-4.* *Storage category link with the external repository*

3. **Configure the document type in the DMS system using t-code DC10.** This document type will be used to identify the attachments for functional locations and notifications.

4. **Define a new document type ZB1.** See Figures 6-5 and 6-6.

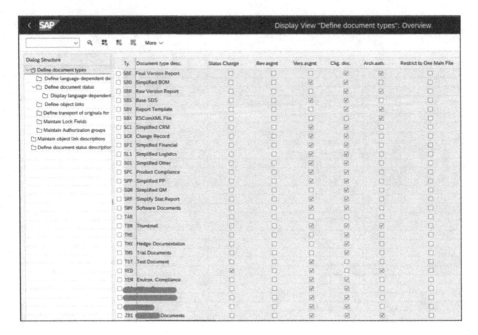

*Figure 6-5. Document types*

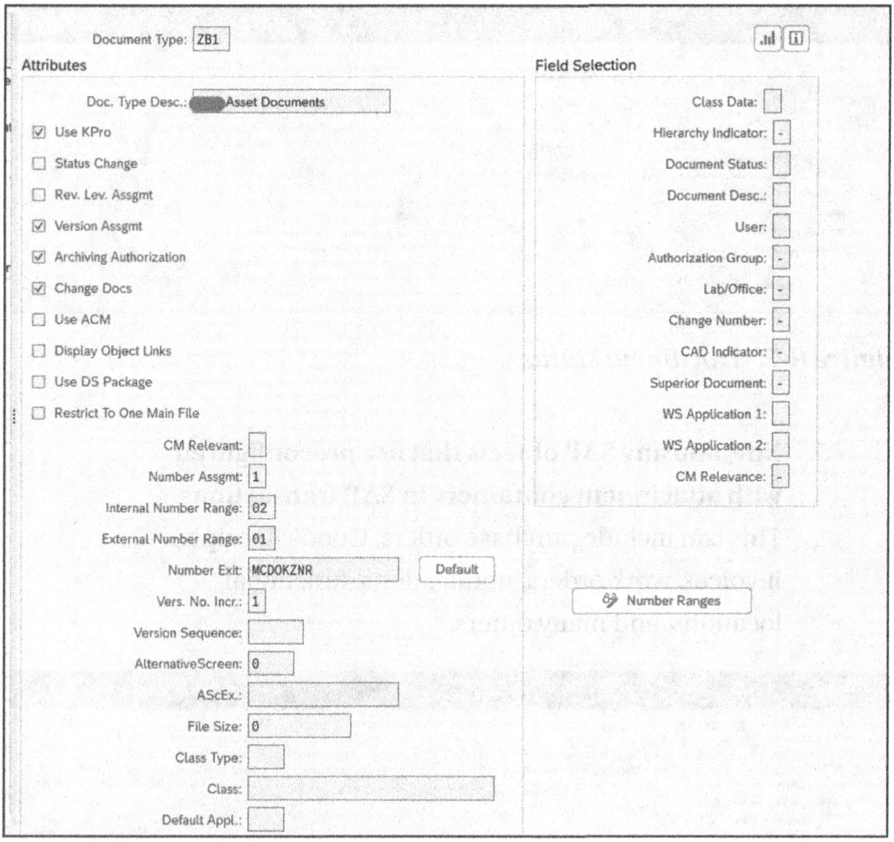

**Figure 6-6.** *Document type details*

This process creates two statuses, called Create and Released. Initially, attached documents will be added in the Create status and then immediately set to the Released status. If you have workflow requirements for document approvals before documents can be published, you can use these statuses to add the workflow.

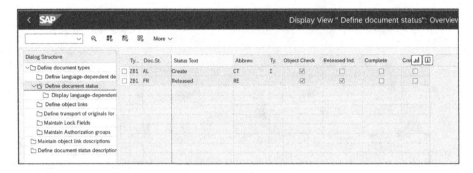

***Figure 6-7.*** *Document status*

> 5. **Now add any SAP objects that are preconfigured with attachment containers in SAP transactions.** This can include purchase orders, Goods Receipts, invoices, work orders, notifications, functional locations, and many others.

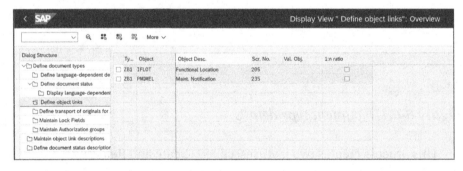

***Figure 6-8.*** *Define object links*

> 6. **Now add the data carrier.** See Figure 6-9.

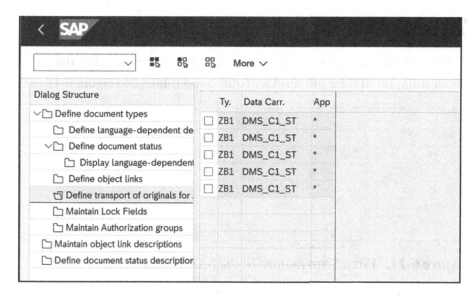

***Figure 6-9.*** *Data carrier*

7. **Next, configure the document extensions that are allowed in the DMS system using t-code DC30.**

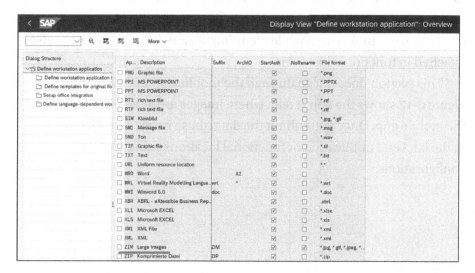

***Figure 6-10.*** *Document extensions*

# Virus Scanning the Attachments

SAP Mobile Services provide virus scanning features that can be enabled at the destination RFC for inbound and outbound traffic. See Figure 6-11.

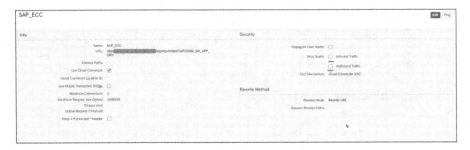

***Figure 6-11.*** *Virus Scan feature in the SAP Mobile Server*

# Attachments in Mobile Apps

This example created a mobile app that's used to capture images for asset inspections. It creates notifications in SAP ECC with maintenance observations and attaches the images in the content repository that are taken from the mobile app while recording observations. Images are also attached in functional locations.

This section does not go through the mobile app functions, but Figure 6-12 shows the app screen where images are attached from the mobile app. Once you submit the data, these images are saved in the backend notification or functional locations using SAP DMS configurations.

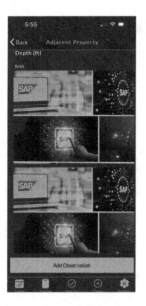

**Figure 6-12.** *Image selection on the mobile application*

Images are attached in the backend notification. The system generates a unique document number in DMS, which is linked to the notification. See Figure 6-13.

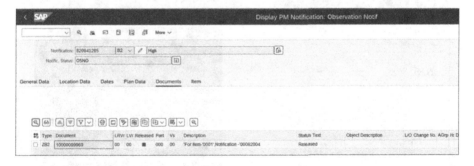

**Figure 6-13.** *Notification screen with the DMS document link*

If you click this document, you can open the images that are saved in the content repository. See Figure 6-14.

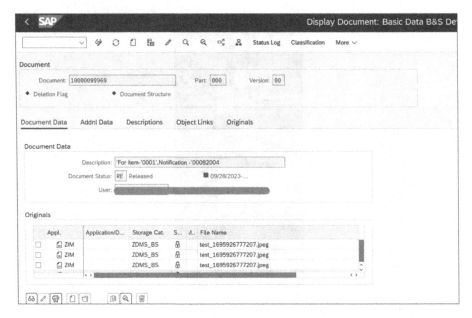

**Figure 6-14.** *DMS document with image list*

This document can be managed from the backend using SAP t-codes **CV01N**, **CV02N**, and **CV03N**. See Figure 6-15.

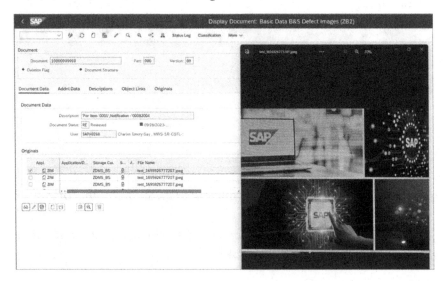

**Figure 6-15.** *DMS document with image details*

SAP has several function modules and BAPIs (Business Application Programming Interfaces) that can be used to create DMS documents, attach files in the repository, and fetch these files from content repositories.

# Testing the Service for Attachment

This example created another service to add images from the mobile app to the functional location for bridges. This process has been divided into two steps.

1.  The first step is to generate document numbers for the images in SAP DMS in Create status.

2.  The second step is to add the images in this document container and release the document so that images can be accessed from the repository.

Figure 6-16 shows how to execute an OData service for document creation in DMS.

```
/sap/opu/odata/sap/ZPM_BS_EXECUTEON_SRV/AssetDockeySet(tplnr
='BRDG002',createFlag='X')?sap-client=100
```

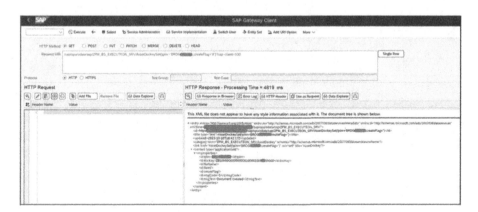

***Figure 6-16.***  *Test OData service for DMS document creation*

Figure 6-17 shows that document number 10000100036 has been generated with Create status and linked with functional location BRDG002.

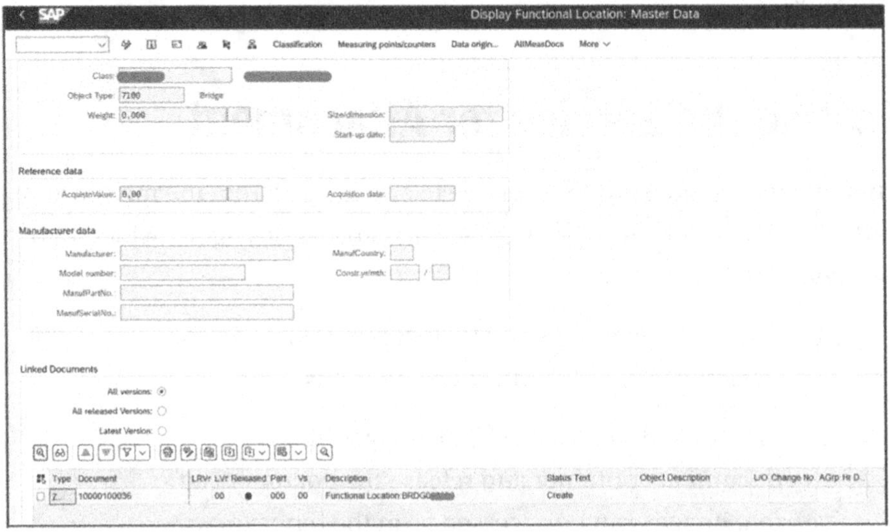

***Figure 6-17.*** *Functional location with DMS document link*

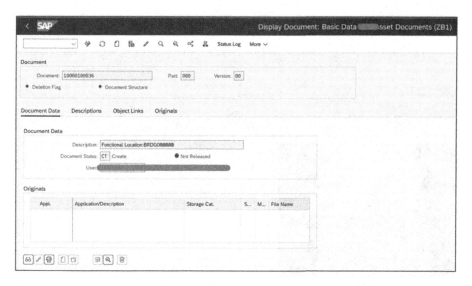

***Figure 6-18.*** *Generated DMS document — create status*

Now you execute OData in the second step to add images to this container. This example converts images to the Xstring format to pass through the OData service.

For testing, the example is from the SAP Gateway Client, and the image is attached as a .jpeg file.

```
/sap/opu/odata/sap/ZPM_BS_SELECTINS_SRV/FileUISet
(racfid='',sourceid='U',appid='SI',dockey=
'ZB10000000000000010000100036000000',filename='IMG_0295.jpeg',
FileId='',DeleteFile='')/$value
```

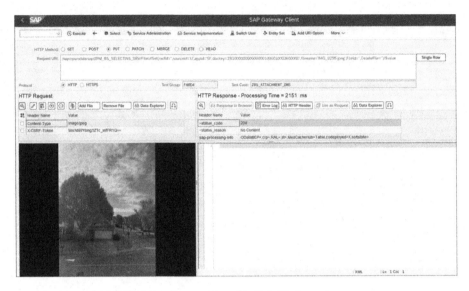

*Figure 6-19.*  *Adding an image to the DMS document*

After a successful run, the image will be added to the DMS document, which is linked to a functional location, and the document will be set to Released status for further use. See Figure 6-20.

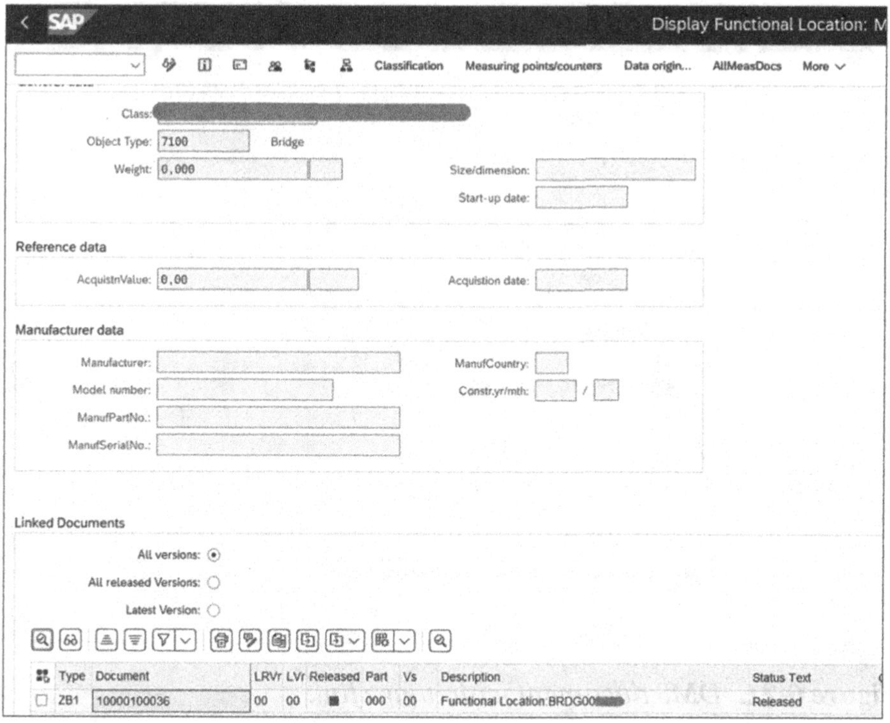

***Figure 6-20.*** *DMS document — release status*

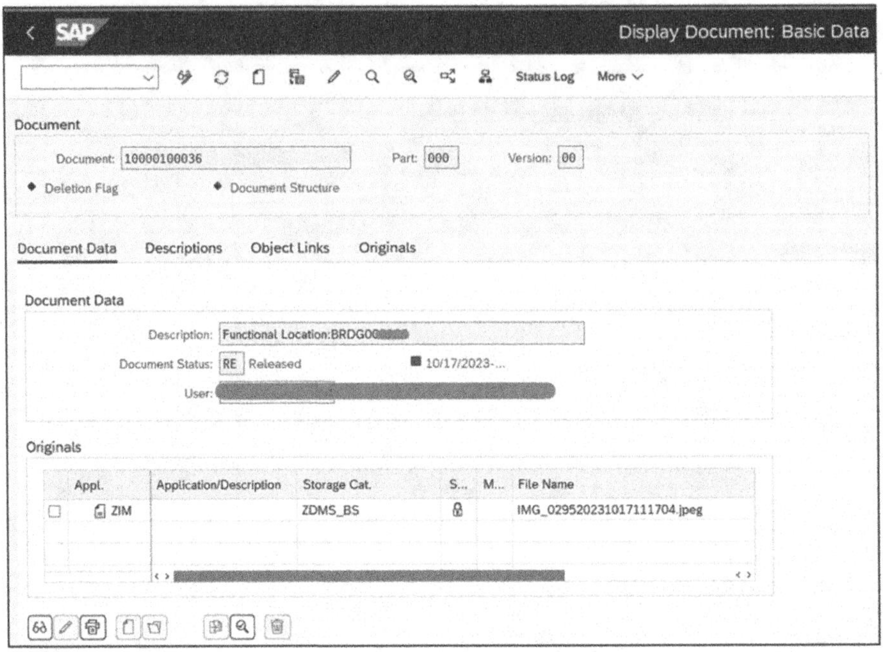

**Figure 6-21.** *DMS document with image link*

The image can be opened from the content repository, as shown in Figure 6-22.

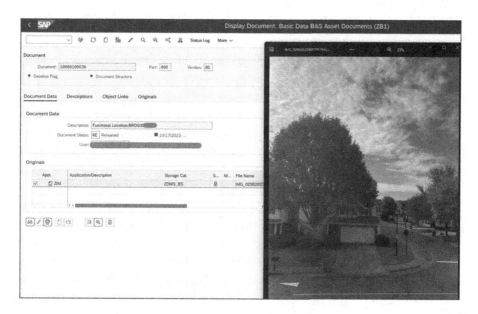

*Figure 6-22.* *DMS document with image detail*

You can use attachment functions as per your application needs for all the supported object types.

# Compressing Images from Mobile Phones

Frequently, you'll need to incorporate attached images into legal documents. Given that modern smartphones capture images in exceptionally high resolution, often surpassing the requirements for business documents, it is often essential to compress these images at the UI/UX layer before transferring them to the content repository.

Prior to incorporating images, it is advisable to compress them. This not only prevents an escalation in database size, but also mitigates potential performance issues during the storage and retrieval of images.

The example code in Figure 6-23 slices the image in 512KB.

```
// Takes a base64 string and converts it into a blob
b64toBlob(b64Data, contentType, sliceSize) {
  contentType = contentType || '';
  sliceSize = sliceSize || 512;
  const byteCharacters = atob(b64Data);
  const byteArrays = [];

  for (let offset = 0; offset < byteCharacters.length; offset += sliceSize) {
    const slice = byteCharacters.slice(offset, offset + sliceSize);
    const byteNumbers = new Array(slice.length);

    for (let i = 0; i < slice.length; i++) {
      byteNumbers[i] = slice.charCodeAt(i);
    }

    const byteArray = new Uint8Array(byteNumbers);
    byteArrays.push(byteArray);
  }

  const blob = new Blob(byteArrays, { type: contentType });
  return blob;
```

***Figure 6-23.*** *Angular code snippets for slicing the image size*

# Bundling and Stitching Method for PDF Documents

Often, you'll need to utilize images stored in a database to generate a PDF document. However, incorporating numerous images into a document can pose challenges. The document size tends to escalate, presenting difficulties in document creation. SAP ADS (Adobe Document Service) may return an error when the document has more than 1000 pages.

SAP allows you to use a stitching method to create a PDF document of more than 1000 pages. This needs to be done in the backend SAP system, where the OData service has been written. The OData service will do the stitching and will produce the final stitched PDF form, which can then be passed to the frontend as a single document. More details about this procedure can be found at this link:

```
https://help.sap.com/docs/SUPPORT_CONTENT/interactiveforms/
3353524583.html
```

This approach utilizes Adobe Document Service (ADS) settings. If ADS is not configured correctly in your SAP system, then you will get an error while running the stitching services.

If you want to understand the process of creating Adobe forms in SAP, check out the details from this link:

```
https://help.sap.com/docs/SUPPORT_CONTENT/interactiveforms/
3353525928.html
```

This chapter does not go through the details of creating Adobe forms. You can see the example code in the SAP report FP_CHECK_BATCH_PDF_ RETURN, which uses the sequence of calls shown in Figure 6-24 for Adobe form functions to bundle all the pages and then stitch them into a single PDF document.

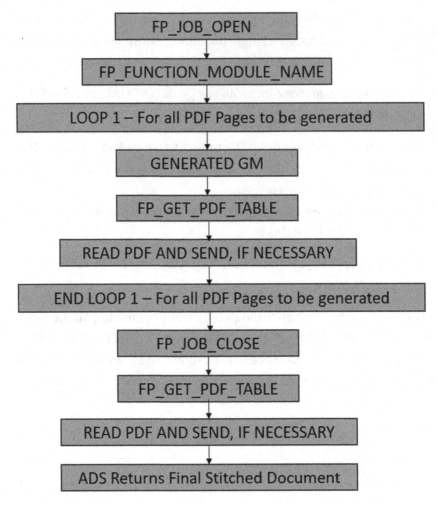

***Figure 6-24.*** *Process flow to stitch multiple PDF forms into one PDF*

The FP_JOB_OPEN function should be called with output parameters, as shown here.

```
CALL FUNCTION 'FP_JOB_OPEN'
    CHANGING
        IE_OUTPUTPARAMS         = FP_OUTPUTPARAMS
    EXCEPTIONS
        CANCEL                  = 1
        USAGE_ERROR             = 2
        SYSTEM_ERROR            = 3
        INTERNAL_ERROR          = 4
        OTHERS                  = 5.
*****
FP_OUTPUTPARAMS -NODIALOG       = 'X'.
FP_OUTPUTPARAMS -GETPDF         = 'M'.
FP_OUTPUTPARAMS -ASSEMBLE       = 'S'.
FP_OUTPUTPARAMS-CONNECTION      = 'ADS'.
FP_OUTPUTPARAMS-BUMODE          = 'M'.
```

Note that ADS is the RFC name for Adobe Document Services.

# Alternative Stitching Method

In addition to the previous approach, you can use the approach in Figure 6-25 to merge multiple PDF pages into a single PDF document. This approach utilizes the SAP-provided class CL_RSPO_PDF_MERGE and its ADD_DOCUMENT and MERGE_DOCUMENTS methods.

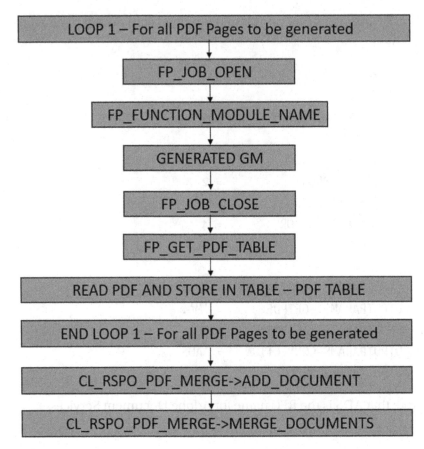

**Figure 6-25.** *Alternative process flow to stitch multiple PDF forms into one PDF*

```
LOOP AT PDF_TABLE INTO lv_pdf_data.
 lo_cl_merge->add_document( lv_pdf_data).
ENDLOOP.

 lo_cl_merge->merge_documents( IMPORTING merged_document =
 lv_merge ).
```

This covers the process of stitching individual PDF pages in one single PDF document, storing and retrieving the documents/images in the SAP DMS server, and sending and receiving them to frontend mobile apps through OData services.

# Index

## A

Adobe Document Service (ADS), 238, 239, 241
Ahead-of-time (AOT), 139
Angular framework, 202
   barcode scanning, 207
   compressing image, 238, 239
   CORS protocol/capacitor
     configuration, 209, 210
   CSRF token, 208
   key features/
     components, 135–137
   print labels, 210–216
   registering/deleting devices
     code snippets, 205
     CREATE method, 203
     DELETE method, 204
     installation process, 203
     mobile server logs, 207
     OData URLs, 206
     steps, 202
Application Programming Interfaces
   (APIs), 57, 141, 231

## B

Barcode scanning, 3, 147, 207
Business Application Programming
   Interfaces (BAPIs), 231

Business Technology Platform
   (SAP BTP)
   benefits, 104
   business user apps, 105
   cloud connector, 107–109
   customer-facing apps, 105
   employee-facing apps, 105
   features, 103, 104
   field service apps, 105
   IoT apps, 105
   mobile service configuration
     basic information, 115
     connectivity
      configuration, 118
     destination/device
      registration, 116
     ECC system, 116, 118
     exchange configuration, 119
     features, 114
     global account/subaccount,
      109, 110
     hybrid mobile
      application, 112
     instance running, 114
     OAuth client/API
      configuration, 115
     role settings, 113
     security settings, 113

© Pranay Gupta 2024
P. Gupta, *Digital Transformation of SAP Supply Chain Processes*,
https://doi.org/10.1007/979-8-8688-0270-6